OSPREY AIRCRAFT OF THE ACES® • 70

F-86 Sabre Aces of the 51st Fighter Wing

SERIES EDITOR: TONY HOLMES

OSPREY AIRCRAFT OF THE ACES® • 70

F-86 Sabre Aces of the 51st Fighter Wing

Warren Thompson

OSPREY
PUBLISHING

FRONT COVER
During the morning of 17 November 1952, World War 2 P-51 Mustang ace Maj Ed Heller claimed his first aerial victory in almost seven years when he downed a MiG-15 near Tangmok-tank, on the North Korea/Manchuria border. Assigned to the 51st FW's 16th FS, and flying F-86E-10 51-2756, Heller was leading his wingman, 1Lt Philip C Davis, on a high-altitude sweep of 'MiG Alley'. The latter pilot takes up the story;

'As a young lieutenant, and wingman, I was privileged to be able to fly with our squadron's future CO, Maj Ed Heller. He was the ultimate fighter pilot, and a great teacher. On this particular mission, one of the pilots in our flight had a hung wing tank, and the rules dictated that he and his wingman leave the patrol and return to base. This left Maj Heller and I as a two-ship. We were at 35,000 ft and headed in the direction of Antung at the time, although we were still south of the Yalu River .

'As we passed the "Mizou" (Suiho Reservoir), we spotted two MiG-15s in relatively close formation just ahead and below us. Heller called the bounce and I assumed the protective position below and aft of him. The major opened up at 800 ft and both MiGs pulled up and to the left, with Heller still firing. He was getting good hits on MiG No 1, which broke left and down, while MiG No 2 continued up and to the left, which was perfect for me to get a shot in. However, as a good wingman, my job was to stay with my lead, and for a split-second I wrestled with this dilemma, before deciding I had better stick to the rules. This proved to be a dumb move.

'MiG No 2 immediately dropped in behind me and started shooting balls of fire in my direction. I pulled up as hard as an F-86 could take without losing it. Hunkering down behind the armour plate behind the seat, I kept repeating to myself, "He can't hit me. He can't hit me", and he didn't. After approximately 720 degrees of high-G turning, I eased up and MiG No 2 was nowhere to be seen. Miraculously, I found Maj Heller as soon as I rolled out, and once I had joined up with him, we headed back to Suwon. My leader had claimed his first MiG kill, and if I'd chosen to break the wingman's code, I might
have got one too. However, my mission priorities were correct'

First published in Great Britain in 2006 by Osprey Publishing
Midland House, West Way, Botley, Oxford, OX2 0PH
443 Park Avenue South, New York, NY, 10016, USA
E-mail: info@ospreypublishing.com

ISBN 1 84176 995 9

Edited by Tony Holmes
Page design by Tony Truscott
Cover Artwork by Mark Postlethwaite
Aircraft Profiles and Line Artwork by Mark Styling
Index by Alan Thatcher
Originated by United Graphics, Singapore
Printed and bound in China through Bookbuilders

06 07 08 09 10   10 9 8 7 6 5 4 3 2 1

For a catalogue of all books published by Osprey please contact:

NORTH AMERICA
Osprey Direct, c/o Random House Distribution Center,
400 Hahn Road, Westminster, MD 21157
E-mail: info@ospreydirect.com

ALL OTHER REGIONS
Osprey Direct UK, P.O. Box 140 Wellingborough,
Northants, NN8 2FA, UK
E-mail: info@ospreydirect.co.uk

Buy online at www.ospreypublishing.com

EDITOR'S NOTE
To make this best-selling series as authoritative as possible, the Editor would be interested in hearing from any individual who may have relevant photographs, documentation or first-hand experiences relating to the world's elite pilots, and their aircraft, of the various theatres of war. Any material used will be credited to its original source. Please write to Tony Holmes via e-mail at:

tony.holmes@osprey-jets.freeserve.co.uk

(Cover Artwork by Mark Postlethwaite)

CONTENTS

INTRODUCTION

The introduction of the North American F-86 Sabre into combat over Korea by the 4th Fighter Wing (FW) in November 1950 (see *Osprey Aircraft of the Aces 72 - F-86 Sabre Aces of the 4th Fighter Wing* for details) was considered a great success, even though the aircraft initially proved maintenance-intensive in the field. However, the increasing number of MiG-15s that had been moved into Manchuria by mid 1951 made the Far East Air Force (FEAF) and the Pentagon realise that air supremacy over the frontlines and critical United Nations (UN) air bases scattered across South Korea could be quickly lost.

Constant monitoring of communist airfields in Manchuria had kept UN commanders abreast of the serious threat posed by the ever-growing MiG-15 force along the North Korean border. And it was a single report produced by USAF intelligence in the autumn of 1951, backed by an anxious plea for help from the CO of the 4th FW, that finally saw the FEAF's request for an additional Sabre wing in-theatre approved by the US government soon after the document had arrived in the Pentagon.

Reconnaissance aircraft had been keeping a close eye on the numerous satellite airfields around Antung (known as the Antung Complex), and photographs from a mission over the Yalu River confirmed that a new fighter aviation regiment had moved in to Takishan air base, bringing the total number of MiG-15s in Manchuria to 290. It was time to respond to the threat, and reinforcements would come not a minute too soon, as subsequent intelligence reports showed that the MiG-15 force ranged against the FEAF actually totalled 400+ jets, opposed by just 89 barely serviceable Sabres (based in South Korea and Japan).

The FEAF's senior war planners asked for sufficient F-86s to equip an additional two wings with Sabres, but approval was received on 22 October 1951 for just 75 jets, which would be allocated to the 51st FW.

When the war started in late June 1950, the F-80 Shooting Star-equipped 51st was based on the Japanese island of Okinawa. Amongst the first USAF units to respond to the crisis in Korea, the wing was alerted for movement from its Naha base to Itazuke, in southern Japan, on 6 September 1950. Here, it would be attached to HQ Fifth Air Force. The 51st subsequently entered combat with only two squadrons (the 16th and the 25th FSs), as it was forced to leave one unit (the 26th FS) intact at Naha to carry on performing the wing's pre-war FEAF mission of providing the air defence of Okinawa and the surrounding area.

In the spring of 1950 there were three wings of F-80s in Japan (the 8th, 35th and 49th Fighter-Bomber Wings) and one on Okinawa (the 51st). Three of these wings would bear the brunt of early air combat in the Korean War, which erupted on 25 June 1950 when North Korean T-34-85 tanks rumbled south across the 38th Parallel and headed directly for Seoul. The 35th FBW was left to perform its air defence of central Japan mission from Johnson AFB, near Tokyo.

The attrition rate with the older F-80s was very high, and the FEAF realised early on that there would not be an endless number of replacement aircraft to keep the units at full strength. This meant that surviving Shooting Stars would funnel into fewer and fewer squadrons, and eventually only one wing – the 8th FBW. With the 49th FBW converting onto the newer F-84 Thunderjet and continuing in its fighter-bomber role in the spring of 1951, the two squadrons of the 51st FW were selected for re-equipment with the new F-86Es that were destined for the FEAF in December of that same year.

F-86Es ENTER COMBAT

The E-model Sabres allocated to the 51st FW were improved versions of the world-beating F-86A. The latter had been in operational service with the USAF since the 1st FG's 94th FS had received its Sabres in February 1949 at March AFB, in California. In February 1951 a superior version of the Sabre began reaching Air Force units in the USA in the form of the F-86E.

Like all good military aircraft manufacturers, North American Aviation was constantly analysing the comments and feedback it received from frontline pilots to find out what they needed to do to make the fighter even better. This information duly resulted in the production of the E-model Sabre, which boasted an 'all-flying tailplane' operated by fully hydraulic actuators to help cure handling woes that pilots reported plagued the F-86A at transonic speed ranges. The new actuators replaced mechanically-adjustable stabilisers that were responsible for trim control in the A-model, the new elevators and horizontal stabilisers now being controlled as one unit. To quote F-86 Sabre expert Ray Wagner;

'The horizontal stabiliser was pivoted at its rear spar so that the leading edge was moved eight degrees up and down by normal control column action. The elevator was mechanically linked to the stabiliser and moved in a specific relationship to stabiliser movement.'

The end result of this modification was an F-86 that had responsive controls and great manoeuvrability even at transonic speeds.

One of the first service pilots to fly the new E-model in the spring of 1951 was Lt Joe Cannon of the 62nd FS/56th FW, and he would subsequently complete more than 40 missions in Korea as wingman to legendary ace, and future commanding officer of both the 4th and 51st FWs, Col Francis 'Gabby' Gabreski. He reflected on the chain of events that led up to the new F-86Es being loaded onto the aircraft carrier USS *Cape Esperance* and shipped to Korea to equip the 51st in the late autumn of 1951;

'While I was flying with the 62nd FS at Chicago O'Hare, we had several future 4th/51st FW aces with us in the squadron – Iven Kincheloe, Don Adams (who taught me how to dogfight in the F-86A over Lake Michigan) and World War 2 ace

16th FS pilot Major Donald Adams climbs out of the cockpit of his F-86E after an encounter with MiG-15s high over the Yalu River during the afternoon of 27 May 1952. He had just claimed his last victory, taking his tally to 6.5 kills. Adams had joined the 51st FW from the 56th FG six months earlier, and had 'made ace' with a double MIG haul on 3 May. Having completed his combat tour on 13 June 1952, Adams returned to the US and joined the F-89-equipped 1st FW. He was subsequently killed in a flying accident in F-89C 51-5781 at Detroit airport on 30 August 1952 (*T R White*)

The first pilot to attain ace status whilst serving with the 51st FW was Maj Bill Whisner, seen here receiving last minute instructions from his crew chief. Having already claimed 15.5 kills with the 352nd FG during World War 2, Whisner scored two MiG-15 victories (and was credited with damaging a further four jets) whilst serving with the 4th FW's 334th FS prior to joining the 51st FW's 25th FS in November 1951. On the afternoon of 23 February 1952 Whisner bagged his fifth MiG, thus taking his tally in Korea to 5.5 victories, and making him the USAF's seventh jet ace (*Iven Kincheloe*)

Having completed strapping in, Maj Whisner prepares to fire up the engine in his F-86E at Suwon in early 1952. His crew chief is keeping a watchful eye on the gauges in the cockpit whilst the pilot runs through the engine ignition sequence (*Bill Nowadnick*)

Bill Whisner, as well as the 56th FW's then CO, "Gabby" Gabreski. I can honestly tell you that there were several other pilots that were of the same calibre as these aces.

'In early 1951, we began ferrying the new F-86Es from the factory in California back to Chicago. Lt Kincheloe and I flew a lot of sorties in both the A- and E-models at this time, and we used to argue with each other about which one of us had the most time in the jet in the Air Force.

'It didn't take long for all of us to realise just how much better the F-86E was in comparison with the F-86A. Its improved handling, thanks to its all-hydraulic controls, really came to the fore during our mock dogfights. For example, in the new model it was very easy to "Split-S" at 40,000 ft and pull out of a vertical dive while going through the speed of sound (Mach 1). This was done with ease through light back pressure on the control column, and we didn't witness any of the violent rolling tendencies that afflicted the F-86A. This was due, in part, to the fact that we had an "all-flying tail", where the entire horizontal tail moved with the stick control instead of just the elevator.

'On the downside, flying formation with the E-model initially proved to be more difficult than it had been in the F-86A due to the sensitivity of the new control system. However, after a few hours of formation time, pilots quickly became comfortable when flying in close proximity to each other.

'The more powerful J47-GE-13 turbojet engine in the F-86E, which produced an extra 600 lbs of thrust, was also a great asset in a dogfight, as was the A-1CM gunsight.'

Getting used to the new Sabre required a certain amount of flight time, and the highly qualified pilots then serving with Col Gabreski's 56th FG quickly adapted to their new mounts. Many of them had World War 2 combat time in their log books, and their aggressive nature and wartime experience ensured that they would make a name for themselves when they were transferred into the 51st FW, along with the new F-86Es.

In late June 1951, the transportation of near-new F-86Es destined for the FEAF began, these aircraft being taken from the US-based 1st and 33rd FWs. The first batch to depart from Naval Air Station Alameda, California, were assigned to the hard-pressed 4th FW in an effort to bolster its strength, while the second shipment of 75 E-models departed from the same naval base aboard the aircraft carriers USS *Cape Esperance* and USS *Sitkoh Bay* on 1 and 9 November, respectively.

The latter jets were ultimately destined for Suwon AB, in Korea, to replace the 51st FW's war-weary F-80Cs.

It should also be mentioned here that the USAF subsequently purchased 60 licence-built F-86E-6s from Canadair to help relieve the over-taxed assembly lines at North American's Inglewood, California, facility. These aircraft, destined for the 51st FW, were delivered to the Air Force between February and July 1952 and fitted with US equipment at the Fresno modification centre in California prior to being shipped to Korea.

Returning to July 1951, Col Gabreski and his 'hand-picked' pilots, pulled from the 56th FW, accompanied the F-86Es across the Pacific. Lt Cannon had vivid memories of the voyage;

'We loaded all of the Sabres from our 62nd FS aboard the *Cape Esperance* for the fast trip over to Japan. We were hit by an enormous typhoon in the middle of the Pacific, and our carrier was so top heavy from the large number of Sabres chained to the flightdeck that we came close to capsizing. It was an unbelievable experience. The salt water all but destroyed the electrical systems of the aircraft that were top side, and this duly meant that we would experience a lot of in-flight emergencies with these jets once we started flying them over "MiG Alley".'

Within weeks of the first F-86Es being issued to the 4th FW, pilots from the wing began encountering a newer and more dangerous version of the MiG fighter, which UN intelligence identified as the MiG-15bis. The new communist interceptor was fitted with the more powerful VK-1 turbojet engine which gave the MiG-15bis a top speed of 688 mph, compared with 652 mph for the RD-45F-powered MiG-15. Its existence in ever-growing numbers in Manchuria only compounded the problems

The aircraft carrier USS *Cape Esperance* had been tasked with getting the first F-86As to the Far East in November 1950, and it was called on again 12 months later to transport the new F-86Es to the 51st FW. These Sabres, strapped and chained down to the carrier's flightdeck, were protected against the elements by a thick coat of anti-corrosion compound (*James Hardin*)

faced by the 4th FW that already existed because of the numerical advantage the older versions had. The answer to this new adversary was the F-86E, which had only been in service with the wing for a matter of weeks. And more were needed if the Sabre pilots were to prevail against odds of ten-to-one in the skies over Korea.

NEW SABRE WING

Once the FEAF received word in October that an additional 75 Sabres would be allocated to the Korean campaign, senior Air Force officers in-theatre set about issuing orders to prepare the 51st FW for its conversion from war-weary F-80Cs to near-new F-86Es. This in turn allowed the wing to establish exactly what its responsibilities would be once it was Sabre-equipped. The 51st's priorities were broken down as follows;

1) the destruction of all enemy airpower over the Korean Peninsula

2) escort duties for all UN military assets, encompassing forces on land, at sea and in the air

3) air defence of all major air bases in South Korea during daylight hours

4) special missions that included search and rescue and top cover for any ground operations that involved extracting downed aircrews from enemy territory

In time of war, there can be no extended period given to assist in a smooth transition from one aircraft type to another. It was a critical situation that the Sabre-equipped 51st FW was now facing, and there was no spare time available for the unit's pilots and maintainers to go through the normal training period that would have been observed had the wing been converting in the USA.

The most important mission entrusted to any of the F-86 wings to see combat in Korea was to help UN forces maintain air superiority in-theatre. Ground forces had depended on support from the skies to help them stem the tide of the Chinese and North Korean advances in late 1950, and the stalemate that now existed was due in no small part to the continued mastery of the skies enjoyed by UN forces throughout 1951.

'Counter-air' missions had been the principal way that the 4th FW had maintained air superiority since arriving in Korea in December 1950, these sorties seeing a countless number of fighter sweeps performed over northwest Korea in an effort to keep the numerically superior MiGs at bay. The 4th had been tasked with acting as a buffer between the enemy fighters and the heavily laden attack aircraft that were going after key targets well within range of the communist fighters. Most of these sweeps were carried out right before the UN attack aircraft reached their target, and the Sabres' pilots usually met with success, despite the employment of new counter counter-air tactics by the MiG-15 pilots.

The re-equipment of the 51st FW would help ease the 4th FW's burden as soon as the wing was deemed ready for combat in December 1951. And like the 4th before it, the 51st was constantly forced to spread out its limited Sabre assets along the Yalu River in order to provide heavy

North American Aviation provided expert help in the field with their small army of Technical Representatives, who helped iron out numerous minor problems with the Sabres throughout their tenure in the Korean War. The individual in the black baseball cap is John Henderson, who travelled to the war zone with the 4th FW as part of the team supporting the F-86A. To his left is 51st FW 'tech rep' James R Moddrell. The backdrop for this photograph is provided by an F-86A of the 4th FW, which dates this shot as having been taken in the summer of 1951 – before the 51st FW had converted from the F-80C to the F-86E (*John Henderson*)

bombers with high altitude cover and, at the same time, low altitude protection for attack aircraft threatened by MiG-15s attempting to penetrate the fighter screen closer to the ground.

Although the 51st's switch from the F-80C to F-86E was eased a little by the fact that the wing was swapping one jet type for another, it still encountered numerous problems which hampered the transition. The first of these was the failure by FEAF HQ to establish dates by which all Shooting Star operations were to cease and Sabre sorties were to start.

The pressure being placed on the fighter-bomber units at this time was excessive, as Chinese forces had recently increased their efforts to re-supply their ground forces in the frontline. The UN, in response, had tasked their ground attack squadrons with negating this push by hitting troop and materiel convoys as they neared their objectives. The 51st's two squadrons of F-80Cs would play a crucial part in reducing the effectiveness of the communist re-supply effort.

The wing's conversion was also severely hampered by the lack of a functioning supply chain to provide spare parts for its new Sabres. This in turn meant that the 51st rarely met its FEAF-stipulated required in-service rate during the wing's early months of F-86 flying. And although the quality of the 'tech reps' furnished by the various manufacturers involved in the building of the Sabre was top notch, the serviceability issues afflicting the aircraft were further exacerbated by the failure of the USAF to provide sufficient copies of the technical orders for the wing's maintenance personnel.

Lastly, there was a dearth of engine build-up kits in-theatre, which seriously limited the supply of replacement powerplants. These problems also afflicted the 4th FW in early 1952, and, in January and February of that year, both wings could only achieve an in-commission rate of 55 per cent, which was well below the acceptable mark expected by the FEAF.

These maintenance woes were the end result of the 51st FW's conversion to the F-86 having not been programmed months in advance, as was usually the case in the Air Force. The wing's hasty swap from Shooting Stars to Sabres in turn placed extreme limitations on the unit's logistics support, and also had a detrimental impact on the number of qualified pilots available to fly those aircraft that could be made serviceable. The shortfall in the latter meant that a number of pilots rotating into the wing had only previously flown piston-engined bombers or multiengined transports! The Sabre-experienced pilots in the 51st therefore spent much of December 1951 training the numerous F-86 novices in the art of flying jet fighters.

As a direct result of the lack of experienced jet pilots in-theatre in early 1952, the FEAF briefly reduced the requirement that all fighter pilots complete 100 missions prior to being declared tour-expired. An 'available-replacement' basis was introduced instead, as the new Sabre pilots brought in from piston-engined types needed considerable extra training in order to be able to survive the high-speed, intense dogfights that they would be involved in. This in turn meant that combat-rated pilots were only getting to fly around ten operational missions per month due to their training commitments, making it almost impossible for them to maintain their combat efficiency.

This situation was finally solved when new pilots started to arrive in Korea directly from the USA, and these individuals were fresh from jet training. With several hundred hours on T-33s, F-80s and F-86s already behind them, they joined the 4th and 51st FWs virtually ready for combat. For the veteran pilots already in-theatre, the arrival of the 'new guys' meant more cockpit time for everyone.

Despite the pilot shortage having been all but solved by March 1952, the 51st FW was still grappling with an overall lack of vital equipment for its F-86Es. The biggest problem facing logistics personnel in those early months of Sabre operations was a shortage of drop tanks in Korea. It was no secret that the F-86 had only a modest range, and that the fighter had no chance of reaching 'MiG Alley' from its bases at Suwon and Kimpo on internal fuel only. The scale of the problem was reflected in FEAF records from December 1951. These state that with the introduction of the 51st FW into the combat air patrol regimen, the added pressure put on both wings to protect the fighter-bombers on their missions north of Pyongyang saw the requirement for external fuel tanks jump by 500 per cent!

It came as no surprise, therefore, that by mid-January 1952 the supply of these tanks in-theatre had been totally exhausted. With the cancellation of Sabre sorties out of the question, the only solution to this problem was for pilots to be restricted in their patrol time through the use of only a single drop tank per mission. This led to a large number of F-86s running out of fuel as they returned home, forcing pilots to dead-stick land their jets at Suwon and Kimpo, and several other bases too. An unlucky few never got this far, having to eject from their otherwise serviceable F-86s south of the bomb line. The loss of such valuable aircraft was particularly hard to take for both the 4th and 51st FWs.

25th FS F-86E-1 50-597 taxies out for a mission over North Korea in early 1952. At this time, there was a brief shortage of external fuel tanks in-theatre, which forced units to use just one per jet. This greatly reduced the amount of time Sabre pilots could spend on patrol over 'MiG Alley'. 50-597 was later passed on to the 16th FS, and it was eventually written off during a sortie on 12 July 1952 (*Bernard Brungardt*)

As mentioned earlier, the motive for hastily getting the F-86E into combat was to oppose the ever increasing numbers of MiG-15s that were being based north of the Yalu River. Fortunately, most of these aircraft usually stayed within the safety of Manchurian airspace, and they rarely ventured too far south. However, the number of recorded missions that they did fly over the extreme portions of north-west Korea was very high – 2336 observed sorties in November 1951 and 3997 the following month.

The increasing audacity of the MiG-15 pilots seemed to coincide with the introduction of the re-equipped 51st FW to combat, which meant that the communist pilots were not fazed by the doubling of Sabre numbers. Indeed, there were two recorded incidents where MiG-15s were sighted close to Seoul (on 3 and 8 December). Of course, these forays were at extreme altitude, and with no indication on either occasion that the pilots had any plans to attack the South Korean capital. North Korean spies captured during this period also confirmed the increasing ability of the communist MiG force when they revealed under interrogation that the training programme for MiG-15 units was producing some excellent pilots. Indeed, the latter were currently being introduced to external drop tanks that would put their jets well within range of all major air bases in South Korea.

FIRST MISSIONS

The 51st FW's 25th FS received its first 20 F-86Es at Suwon in mid November 1951, whilst its sister-squadron – the 16th FS – was issued with the next 19 to reach the wing shortly afterwards. Further deliveries were split equally between the two units from then on.

The first official combat sorties flown by the 51st occurred on 1 December 1951 when the 25th FS sent several flights north on fighter sweeps of Sinanju and Chongju – favourite haunts for MiG-15 pilots. The first mission was led by newly-arrived wing commander, Col 'Gabby' Gabreski, and his deputy wing commander, Lt Col George L Jones. Both men had been trans-ferred in from the 4th FW in November 1951, where they had enjoyed success in aerial combat against the growing MiG threat.

Already a 28-kill ace P-47 Thun-derbolt ace from World War 2, Gabreski had downed three MiG-15s during his short spell with the 4th FW, whilst Jones (who had also

Virtually every fighter/fighter-bomber unit that served in Korea had its own gaudily painted mobile control vehicle. This Dodge T214 ³/₄-ton truck, fitted with covered body work, was perfect for this role, as it could be manned in virtually any type of weather. The F-86E taxiing behind it is a 25th FS jet (*Bernard Brungardt*)

Finishing World War 2 as the USAAF's ranking P-47 ace with 28 victories, Francis 'Gabby' Gabreski made the switch to jets in the late 1940s. He duly saw more combat in Korea, firstly with the 4th FW (with whom he claimed two MiG-15 kills in F-86As), and then as the first CO of the 51st FW once it had re-equipped with F-86Es. Leading the wing from 6 November 1951 through to 13 June 1952, Col Gabreski flew F-86E-10 51-2746 *LADY FRANCES* for much of this time. He became the wing's second ace on 13 April 1952. 51-2746 was lost in combat with MiG-15s on 21 November 1952 (*USAF*)

Sabre ace Lt Col George Jones heads for the runway at Suwon in a 25th FS machine at the beginning of yet another combat mission in early 1952. Having begun his combat tour in Korea with the 4th FW (with whom he claimed 1.5 kills), Jones transferred to the 51st FW in November 1951 and added two more kills to his tally in January 1952. He returned home three months later, only to be posted back to the 4th FW's 335th FS in January 1953 as leader of Project *Gunval* (the testing of F-86Fs fitted with 20 mm cannon). Jones would down two and two shared MiG-15s during the *Gunval* deployment, taking his final tally to 6.5 kills and five damaged (*Robert Moddrell*)

Lt Gen Frank F Everest (Fifth Air Force commander) presents an award to Capt Iven Kincheloe soon after he had claimed his fifth kill on 6 April 1952. To Everest's left is 51st FW CO, Col Francis Gabreski. The tenth USAF jet ace, Kincheloe was the first to claim five kills with the 51st FW (*Bill Nowadnick*)

flown P-47s during the final months of the Pacific campaign) had scored 1.5 kills. Great pilots and leaders, both Gabreski and Jones would subsequently attain jet ace status in Korea.

These glories lay ahead for the 51st, however, as the 1 December mission proved to be relatively uneventful, with no claims being made by the wing. Indeed, only three MiG-15s were destroyed on this day, two of which were credited to Meteor F 8s of the Royal Australian Air Force's No 77 Sqn and the third to a 36th FBS/8th FBW F-80C.

The following day the new Sabre wing sortied as many of its aircraft as it could in a major fighter sweep, but once again only a handful of MiGs were spotted. However, 25th FS pilot 1Lt Paul F Roach succeeded in scoring the wing's first kill when he shot one of the enemy fighters down. Another veteran pilot drafted in from the 4th FW, Roach had previously shared in a MiG kill while flying with the 334th FS from Kimpo on 25 September – he would score his final kill with the 25th FS on 28 December. Roach was one of a handful of pilots that Col Gabreski brought with him from the 4th when he moved to Suwon, the veteran ace handpicking more than a dozen aviators to accompany him to the 51st.

Needless to say, the competition between both Sabre wings was fierce virtually from day one, with the 4th and 51st FWs aggressively striving to claim the highest number of victories on a daily basis. Initially, the 4th had the edge thanks to the larger number of Sabres it had on strength and the better luck it enjoyed when searching out MiGs over northern Korea. Between 2 and 12 December, the wing would be credited with 21 straight kills and the 51st just one – Roach's on the 2nd.

Finally, on the 13th, the Gabreski wing ended its run of bad luck when 1Lt Anthony Kulengosky shot down the 51st's second MiG-15. As with Roach, Kulengosky had been brought in from the 4th FW, with whom he had shot down a MiG-15 while flying with the 336th FS on 16 October – he would claim his third, and final, kill on 25 January 1952.

1Lt Joe Cannon was yet another of Col Gabreski's pick-ups from the 4th FW involved in these early missions, and he would fly wing for all four of the future aces that joined the 51st FW from the pioneer Sabre wing in late 1951. Here, he recalls an early spring 1952 mission where he flew as wing-man for 1Lt Iven Kincheloe during a huge dogfight that eventually resulted in Cannon being shot down soon after he had destroyed a MiG-15;

'The MiG-15 could out-perform the F-86E in several aspects with the exception of a vertical dive, where the air speed went to Mach 1. This edge in performance was due to its light weight and a powerful engine that had initially been developed by Rolls-Royce. The MiG could out climb and out turn us, and you had to hang in until you could get the jet in a dive. Many times I saw the wings and tail assembly break off the MiG in high-speed dives.

'On 2 April 1952, over the Yellow Sea, I came up behind a MiG-15 at close range and fired a burst causing it to explode. Seconds later, another MiG shot me down. At 30,000 ft, I "Split-S'd" and banked to the right after I passed through 15,000 ft. Seconds later I lost my hydraulic system, leaving me with no controls in a vertical dive. Thank God North American designed the system to lock the tail (horizontal stabiliser) in the nose high position, and this pulled me out of the dive just before I hit the water. I could not move the stick.

'As my jet began to climb, I realised that I was headed north, and this would have taken me deep into enemy territory. The only thing I could do was stand on the rudder pedals, as there was a cable connection to the tail, and gradually my F-86 skidded around until it was headed south. Performing this turn wore me out, and I was weakened for what was to come.

'Having gained enough altitude to bail out, I ejected and deployed my parachute. As I floated down, several MiGs were trying to make firing passes at me. 1Lt Kincheloe was doing everything he could to divert their attention, and I kept my 'chute swinging as much as I could to make it more difficult to hit me. I popped the air bottle for my Mae West before I hit the water, and also released my 'chute canopy – it is impossible to judge height over open water – so I must have fallen 50 ft before I hit the sea. You had to be sure and release the 'chute canopy prior to landing in the water, for if it came down on top of you, you would drown!

'I came back up for air and realised that I had packed so much in my escape kit that was strapped to my 'chute harness that the Mae West would not keep my head above water. The water was very cold, and in a short time my hands could not feel anything, and I was unable to release the heavy kit from my 'chute straps around my legs.

'In between my many trips up to gasp for air, I saw a rescue chopper

1Lts Curtis 'Dad' Eskew (left) and Joe Cannon (centre) prepare to board a C-46 with Capt Kincheloe (right) for some 'rest & recreation' in Japan in the early spring of 1952. 1Lt Cannon frequently flew wing for both Kincheloe and Col Gabreski (*Iven Kincheloe*)

Capt Iven Kincheloe (left) and Maj Don Rodewald pose for the camera alongside the former's Sabre, F-86E-10 51-2731 *"IVAN"*. Although its pilot spelt his christian name with an 'e', rather than an 'a', the jet's nickname was inexplicably spelt *"IVAN"*. Having survived the war, Kincheloe became a test pilot, and he was killed when his F-104A (56-772) crashed at Edwards air force base on 26 July 1958 (*Iven Kincheloe*)

on the way to get me, so then I knew that Kincheloe had gotten the word to them. Somehow, I had been wounded, and I do not know if it had been in the cockpit or when I ejected. My rescue was successful, and I eventually returned to my base at Suwon. My gun camera film had gone down with my Sabre, and the fight was so intense that I could not prove that I had downed the MiG.

'Fortunately, when I got back I was able to fly many more sorties, and I ended up with 91 combat missions over North Korea to my credit. I eventually flew the F-86H in the reserves, and that was the most impressive Sabre model of all.'

SABRE MARKINGS

During the 51st FW's first few months of operations, the wing's groundcrewmen had little spare time available to adorn the vertical stabilisers of their jets with unit markings, so they were left unpainted. Indeed, the only theatre-specific marking applied to the natural metal Sabres was the FEAF yellow band painted around the fuselage behind the canopy. This would soon change, however, as the wing adopted its famous checker tail design in early 1952. Until then, however, it was probably difficult for communist intelligence operatives to determine exactly which units its MiG-15s were fighting against, although there was no doubt north of the Yalu River that a second Sabre wing had come into theatre!

As the plain F-86Es of the 51st completed more missions in the final weeks of 1951, the experience level of all of Col Gabreski's pilots increased significantly, and by the end of December three more 25th FS pilots had claimed kills, bringing the first month's total to five.

Iven Kincheloe poses for USAF photographers at Suwon soon after he became an ace with the 25th FS. Note that the pilot's helmet has been adorned with the squadron's emblem (*Harry Shumate*)

F-86E-6-CAN 52-2881 of the 25th FS was photographed at altitude en route to 'MiG Alley' during a routine combat air patrol. This shot was taken during the early Gabreski era, when the 51st FW jets had no markings on their vertical stabilisers (*Walt Copeland*)

In this undated still taken from the camera gun fitted to a 51st FW jet, a doomed MiG-15 has suffered a series of strikes that have caused its undercarriage to flop open. Note the burst of 0.50-cal rounds hitting up high on the jet's vertical stabiliser (*USAF*)

The most significant Sabre statistics were posted right after December's victory totals were in. With two wings in operation, the F-86 force in the FEAF had reached 165 (still far below the number of MiGs that were based north of the Yalu River in Manchuria). Of the new Sabre total, 127 were stationed at Kimpo and Suwon and the remaining aircraft were in Japan.

Tensions had continued to mount over 'MiG Alley', as indicated by the F-86 sortie totals for December, which had risen from 1003 in November to 2066. However, this was countered by MiG-15 sorties, which had increased from 2326 to 3997 during the same period. The stage was set for some of the biggest jet air battles of the war.

The 51st FW found itself in the middle of the burgeoning aerial campaign in the New Year, and between 23 and 25 January the wing's pilots were credited with shooting down nine MiG-15s. This boosted the unit's monthly tally to 27, and this would remain the 51st's highest victory return until June 1953, when it would chalk up 29 MiG-15 kills.

Enemy formation strengths and tactics varied widely during the early weeks of 1952, and USAF intelligence officers struggled to get a grip on exactly what the MiG units were doing, or what they were ultimately trying to achieve, as a result. At the time, the UN still believed that all MiG-15s in-theatre were manned by either North Korean or Chinese pilots. However, long after the war had ended, information reached the west which proved this assumption to be very wrong. A significant number of the MiG-15s being encountered over the Yalu River in 1951-52 were being flown by combat-seasoned Soviet pilots.

Relying on their considerable MiG-15 experience, the Soviet pilots would sortie across the Manchurian border into North Korea in large numbers at low level and at a high mach number in an effort to attack the heavily-laden UN fighter-bombers before the F-86 screens could in turn intercept them. Missions employing these tactics were regularly flown by the MiG units between December 1951 and April 1952, the communists exclusively attacking UN aircraft that were conducting bombing missions far north of Pyongyang. By restricting themselves to targeting fighter-bombers in northern Korea, MiG pilots had the chance to then dash back to the safety of Manchuria before patrolling F-86s could get into position to effect an interception.

Towards the end of each month, MiG-15 pilots would also fly south of the Yalu in large numbers at high altitude (45,000 ft+), which put them out of reach of intercepting F-86A/Es. Much later in the war, USAF Intelligence personnel determined that these formations were made up of North Korean and Chinese pilots undergoing conversion training, and the more inexperienced they were, the higher they flew so as to eliminate the chances of having to fight the vastly more experienced Sabre pilots.

ESCALATING MISSION TEMPO

fter several weeks of intense combat flying as wingmen for the older 'heads', most of the F-86 pilots newly assigned to the 51st FW had become well versed in countering the MiG-15 threat by early 1952. Although the pace of the aerial action over 'MiG Alley' seemed to be escalating daily, Sabre pilots still found time to talk tactics and verbally compare their fighters with those of their adversaries.

So far, all of the encounters experienced by the 51st FW had placed them at a great disadvantage, and although most USAF pilots claimed that the Sabre was superior, others maintained that the MiG-15 when flown by an experienced pilot was the better fighter. The facts spoke for themselves – the MiG-15 was lighter and had a more powerful engine, and the combat sorties typically flown by the communist pilots were very short in length. This allowed them more time over the fighting area, whereas the F-86 pilots were at the extreme limit of their range.

The Sabre was also was much heavier than the MiG-15, and could take more punishment. This suited the pilots that flew it, and they would never have been in favour of trading armour for range. The Sabre also had six rapid-firing machine guns as opposed to the three slow-firing cannon fitted to the MiG. The only thing that the Sabre pilots indicated that they would have liked to have seen added to their jet were rapid-firing cannon, which would have given them more knock-down power. This was not

As this photograph clearly shows, when the 51st FW received its first F-86Es in late 1951 the jets were devoid of any identification markings on the vertical stabilisers, although they did boast the theatre-wide yellow and black fuselage band. Taxiing out closest to the camera is 16th FS F-86E-10 51-2762 *Elsie*, which was assigned to Col Clay Tice (who had served as CO of the P-38-equipped 49th FG in World War 2). This aircraft was subsequently written off in an operational accident on 5 June 1953 (*Carl Stewart*)

Seen just days after their delivery to Suwon, these brand new F-86E-10s gave the 51st FW its full complement of aircraft following their arrival in-theatre in early 1952. Their plain vertical stabilisers would soon be adorned with the wing's trademark 'checker tail' marking (*Curtis Eskew*)

possible at the time, but a top secret test of this concept (Project *Gunval*) would have its day in Korea in 1953.

One of the pilots involved in *Gunval* was Lt Col George L Jones, who Col 'Gabby' Gabreski had hand-picked to accompany him to the 51st FW from the 4th FW. The latter was a close friend of Maj Bill Whisner, who was also selected by Gabreski to join the new wing. Like their CO, both of these pilots had seen considerable action flying fighters with the USAAF in World War 2, and they were well on their way to becoming aces in Korea when they arrived at Suwon. Having completed his tour with the 51st FW in April 1952, Jones would rotate back to Korea in January 1953 as part of the top secret *Gunval* project, which used F-86Fs experimentally fitted with 20 mm cannon instead of the 0.50-cal machine guns.

Having joined the 51st FW with 1.5 kills to his credit from his brief time flying F-86As with the 4th FG, Jones damaged a further three MiG-15s during December 1951 sorties with the 51st FW before claiming victories on 12 and 15 January 1952. A flight leader, Jones seemed to have the unfortunate knack of getting tangled up with MiG-15s flown by combat-experienced instructor pilots, known as 'honchos' to the Americans. Here, Jones recalls one such mission in early 1952 where the enemy was exceptionally aggressive, and individual dog-fights were fought out over a vast area. He believed that most of these exceptional pilots were probably Russian or East German, and, like him, they had seen extensive combat in World War 2;

'From time to time in the curious air war over Korea, you met a MiG-15 pilot that possessed exceptional skills. We referred to them as "honchos", and being masters of air tactics, they were very dangerous to go up against. Their nationality was not known at the time, and it remained a mystery for decades after the war. I can tell you that any Sabre pilots that locked horns with this elite bunch never forgot the encounter!

'On this cold, clear day in early 1952, our mission was to fly top cover for some of the new F-84s that were hitting targets a few miles south of the Yalu River. Our briefing officer told us to expect heavy resistance from the MiGs. I was leading two flights of four Sabres, and each flight was separated by about five minutes. This enabled the last flight to stay out of sight, and if the lead group got jumped, they could be in the thick of the fight within a couple of minutes.

'Just about the time we reached our patrol area, the fighter-bomber guys started arriving for their bombing runs. Our contact was watching to see if there was any activity coming from Antung or the airfields nearby. It didn't take long for him to come on the radio and let us know that a large number of MiGs were launching. Peering into the distance towards the airfields, we could see huge clouds of dust being stirred up by the taxiing enemy fighters. Within a few minutes we saw glints of silver reflecting the sunlight, and there were too many of them to even consider counting. As they launched, they pointed their noses almost straight up as they climbed for the altitude advantage.

'The enemy fighters wasted no time playing around north of the river because our fighter-bombers had already started blasting their targets. Someone called out for us to break just as big orange balls of fire came through our loose formation.

World War 2 ace Maj William T Whisner (right) also achieved ace status in jets when he claimed a MiG-15 destroyed on the afternoon of 23 February 1952 whilst serving with the 25th FS. Seen here posing with Capt Utterback at Suwon in December 1951, Maj Whisner already had two kills to his credit flying F-86As with the 334th FS when he had transferred to the 51st FW just weeks prior to this shot being taken (*Iven Kincheloe*)

Photographed on the 25th FS flightline at Suwon, Lt Col George L Jones (left) congratulates 1Lt Cliff Brossart on claiming his second kill on 27 December 1951. The latter pilot had previously shared in the destruction of a MiG-15 on 16 October 1951 whilst flying with the 334th FS. Although Brossart would subsequently fail to add to his tally, Lt Col Jones would become the USAF's 30th jet ace with 6.5 kills on 7 April 1953 (*Iven Kincheloe*)

'The first group of MiGs had gotten the altitude advantage and had come in fast out of the sun to hit us. They were extremely aggressive, and they knew that if they did not take out the top cover Sabres, they would have no chance of getting to the fighter-bombers. As I broke to the right, an all-silver MiG passed in front of me, and it happened so fast that I could not react in time to get behind him. Once he bottomed out of his dive, he went into a steep climb to get back up above us. The performance of the lightweight Russian fighter left it in a league of its own when it came to climbing for altitude! Even though I only made eye contact with my foe for a split-second, I do remember its markings – the fighter's nose and vertical stabiliser were both bright red.'

51st FW commander Col Francis Gabreski chomps on his trademark cigar whilst going through his pre-flight checklist at Suwon in early 1952. Having shot down 28 German fighters in the ETO during World War 2, 33-year-old Gabreski added a further 6.5 MiG-15s to his tally between 8 July 1951 and 13 April 1952 (*Phil Norton*)

It is hard to visualise a high-speed dogfight of more than 100 swept-wing jets taking place in such a confined space. There were probably several mid-air collisions during the course of some of these clashes, but very few were reported. This was probably due to the fact that each pilot was fighting for his life, and therefore had very little time to see what was going on around him other than to the immediate front and rear of his jet. In the wake of these battles, pilots regularly reported that the sky would suddenly empty of aircraft within just a matter of seconds, having previously been full of twisting MiG-15s and F-86s.

There were numerous incidents where the USAF's core leader/wingman elements were split up in the confusion and turmoil, and each Sabre flew back to base with a jet from another flight for company, or the pilot simply returned alone.

The strategy of staggering the arrival times of flights heading into 'MiG Alley' helped break up many of these dogfights, and allowed the Sabre pilots to escape south, despite the enemy outnumbering the F-86 force.

Lt Col Jones continues;

'Soon after spotting the silver and red MiG-15 at close quarters, several more flights from the 51st FW arrived to join the fray, and the sky became even more jammed up with individual dogfights. It was every element for

Two 51st FW aces pose for a third ace. Maj Donald Adams (6.5 kills) and Capt Robert H Moore (5 kills) smile for the camera of Capt Iven Kincheloe (5 kills) at Suwon in early 1952. All three pilots had achieved ace status by early May 1952 whilst flying under the leadership of Col Gabreski (*Iven Kincheloe*)

itself! My wingman and I stuck to a high mach number, as we knew that we had to keep our speed up if we wanted to survive. If you allowed your speed to drop, you were a sitting duck for several MiGs.

'All of a sudden, my wingman called out to break left, and as I did so a MiG streaked by. For some reason or another, he did not fire at me. I rolled over after him as he was close to bottoming out of his dive, and my closure was good. In a matter of seconds I figured I would have a chance

to shoot him down. The pilot must have glanced back and noticed how close I was because he immediately initiated a sharp left turn, increasing his airspeed. By now our altitude was extremely low (about 5000 ft), considering that the fight had started up above 35,000 ft. The number of Gs that I was pulling was getting on up there, yet I still could not pull a lead on him as he continued to increase the distance between us.

'At that time, my wingman called out that we had just passed north of the Yalu River, and at the speed that we were flying, it would not have taken us long to penetrate deep into Manchuria. If we had continued in this direction we would have had insufficient fuel to get home. We were getting close to "bingo" (low fuel, go home time), so I broke it off.

'I looked around and the sky was empty as far as the eye could see. One minute before it had been filled with individual dogfights, yet now the only aircraft I could see was flown by my wingman. I saw no parachutes or billowing smoke coming from the ground, which would have indicated crashed aircraft. The flight back proved to be uneventful. We had been shot at several times, but no shells had come close enough to cause us concern. Although no 51st FW pilots had scored on that mission, there were plenty of other days when we enjoyed better luck.'

COMBAT FRUSTRATION

During the first four months of the 51st FW's time with the Sabre, there was far more frustration than satisfaction for pilots when it came to MiG activity. Even though the overall kill tallies for both Sabre wings for January (32), February (17) and March (39) 1952 were good, for weeks at a time MiG-15s would fly south of the Yalu River in large gaggles at altitudes well beyond the reach of the Sabres, refusing to come down and fight. Day after day, formations of between 100 and 200 communist jets would follow this same routine, frustrating their USAF opponents.

With topped off external tanks, and all boasting the 51st FW's distinctive 'checker tail' marking, this flight of Canadair-built F-86E-6s heads north to 'MiG Alley' on a combat patrol. These aircraft often acted as a buffer for fighter-bombers working over targets along the Yalu River in 1952-53, the MiG-15s having to penetrate the Sabre screen before they could get to the vulnerable attack aircraft (*Cecil Foster*)

Members of the three-nation UN Inspection Team (left) check 51st FW aircraft coming in and out of Korea. This routine was observed throughout the war (*Carl Stewart*)

Maj Donald E Adams was one of the many sharpshooters to serve with the 51st FW. He was credited with shooting down 6.5 MiG-15s between 20 January and 27 May 1952, becoming the USAF's 14th jet ace in the process (*Richard Schoeneman*)

In addition to being out of range, the enemy fighters were hurtling along at about 0.99 mach. And even if the Sabres had been able to reach their altitude (some MiG-15s were flying at 50,000+ ft) and match their speed, it would have been a risky proposition to intercept them because the enemy usually had one section flying below the contrails and another patrolling above the 'cons'. For the Sabre pilots, however, the only MiGs visible to them from their lower altitude were the ones creating the vapour trails.

The 51st FW's newer F-86Es could certainly climb higher than the older A-models, but they still lacked the power to get much beyond 50,000 ft. Desperate to engage the enemy, the Sabre pilots would climb up to their maximum altitude below the MiG formations and track along in the same direction as their opponents in the hope that some aircraft would be lured down to fight. This tactic very seldom worked, however, as the student pilots flying most of the MiG-15s in these formations were under strict orders not to break ranks.

Despite this frustration, the overall results posted by the newer E-model in combat gave credibility to the fact that the 4th FW needed to receive better versions of the Sabre as soon as possible. In January 1952, for example, the 4th's pilots only received credit for the destruction of five of the 32 kills claimed that month – the rest went to the 51st FW. The enhanced performance of the F-86E was clearly the key to defeating the improved MiG-15bis. Indeed, several of Col Gabreski's pilots reinforced this point by stating that they were able to make effective high astern attacks against jets that were caught flying at a slightly lower altitude thanks to the Sabre giving them an altitude advantage in the first place.

Communist pilots soon caught on to the fact that there was a new Sabre in-theatre, and that it could fly much higher than the older F-86A.

Lt Col Albert S Kelly was one of the wing's seasoned veterans who took advantage of the E-model's performance at altitude. Credited with shooting down 2.5 MiG-15s while flying with the 25th FS, he completed more than 100 combat missions;

'We had been on a fighter sweep up along the Yalu and had run into absolutely nothing in the way of something to shoot at! The mission had been very dull. Well into the patrol, one of our guys called out "bingo", so we all made a turn to the south in order to head back to Suwon. At that moment the sky started raining drop tanks! As I looked up, there were three flights of four MiGs bouncing us. We had not seen them, and they must have been at 50,000 ft, as we were cruising around at 38,000 ft.

'Anyhow, we broke up into elements and started climbing to meet them. We got into one hell of a gaggle, with all of us getting split up. There were Sabres and MiGs all over the place. Everyone was yelling at the same time, "Break Right! Break Left!". You could not tell who was telling who what to do. I looked around and my wingman was gone.

I figured that he had taken off after one of the MiGs. My head was on a swivel, and it was a good thing that I looked back when I did because there was a MiG getting ready to tee off on me. He was very close.

'I executed a "split-S", heading straight down for the deck. What seemed like seconds later, I pulled out about ten feet above the water. Levelling off, I glanced back again and that SOB was still on my tail! The only thing I could do was honk my F-86 around in a hard left turn and just keep it at full throttle in the hope that the MiG pilot could not turn with me. I was pulling so many Gs that I figured my G-suit was going to pop. We were somewhere around the mouth of the Yalu, going around and around, when suddenly my radio came on and another Sabre pilot told me. "Hey! That MiG that was on your tail just stalled out and hit the water". Fortunately, I had a witness, so my kill was confirmed. Needless to say, there was a good party at the 51st bar that night!'

A more capable fighter when operated at high altitudes, the MiG-15 was at a disadvantage when it descended below 40,000 ft. Both novice and veteran communist pilots were fully aware of this, and the arrival of the F-86E in Korea only exacerbated the problem. The solution was to order the MiG units to patrol at even higher altitudes, thus keeping out of the range of the Sabre's guns.

With fewer communist fighters being shot down, numbers north of the Yalu River grew rapidly. Intelligence data gathered in February 1952 stated that 540 MiG-15s were based in southern Manchuria, and this estimate proved to be correct. Further north still, beyond the range of UN photo-reconnaissance jets but well within flying distance of 'MiG Alley', there were still more Russian-built fighters. Concerns within the FEAF grew by the week in early 1952 due to these intelligence reports.

During the first seven days of February there were a few instances where MiG-25s were sighted at 53,000 ft. No UN aircraft in-theatre could intercept enemy jets at this altitude, thus allowing the communists to launch a surprise attack south of the 38th Parallel literally at will.

With most of the MiG trains flying at ceilings in excess of 45,000 ft, the F-86 wings had a poor month in February, with the 4th FW only downing six aircraft and the higher-flying 51st FW just 11.

By June 1952, the number of E-models in Korea had boosted the theatre inventory up to the point that the FEAF was able to hold a 50 per cent reserve in Japan. The creation of the latter was helped by the arrival of 60 Canadian-built F-86E-6s in the early spring.

At this time Fifth Air Force commander Lt Gen Frank F Everest announced that he was going to bolster the 51st FW's fighting strength by transferring in a third squadron. He chose the 39th FS, which had been flying F-51Ds in combat as part of 18th FBW at Chinhae AB. Fortunately for the 39th FS, it joined the 51st FW (on 1 June) just as the first big-engined F-86Fs were

Maj William Whisner of the 25th FS strikes a fighter pilot's pose whilst sat in his F-86E-10 51-2735. The USAF's seventh jet ace, he claimed 5.5 MiG-15s to add to his World War 2 tally of 15.5 victories (USAF)

arriving at Suwon, and the unit became the first recipient of the new fighter. This gave the 39th FS pilots a great advantage over their contemporaries flying the A- and E-models.

As the number of F-86Fs increased during the summer of 1952, the 4th FW's highest scoring squadron – the 335th FS – began receiving examples in September 1952. The June/July 1952 period proved to be an historic one for the USAF, for as well as the arrival of the superb F-86F in-theatre, aerial refuelling was introduced into the frontline, thus giving the Air Force the mobility and strike capabilities that it maintains to this day. The first unit to take advantage of aerial refuelling was the 31st Fighter Escort Wing (SAC), which flew its F-84Es from Turner AFB, Georgia, to Japan via the Pacific. This event did not get the media attention that the new F-86F received upon its arrival in Korea, however.

A veteran of a previous combat tour in F-51Ds, 1Lt Charles Gabriel claimed two MiG-15 kills with the 16th FS in the autumn of 1952. Aside from being a successful fighter pilot, Gabriel later went on to become a four-star general and the USAF's 11th Chief of Staff in July 1982. This photograph was taken at Suwon soon after he had claimed his second MiG-15 kill (*Joe Caple*)

IMPROVED SABRE

Based on combat experiences from Korea, North American Aviation and high-ranking Air Force generals in the Pentagon were constantly looking for ways to increase the performance of the F-86. One of the main suggestions coming from both sources was to lower the Sabre's air resistance or 'drag'. Originally, the fighter had been designed with leading edge slats which aerodynamically extended or retracted. These reduced stalling speeds for landing when extended and increased interception speeds when retracted. The slats had been devised by German engineers in World War 2 as they set about lowering the stalling speeds associated with their revolutionary swept wing designs.

In an effort to boost the F-86F's top end performance, North American Aviation technicians sealed the slats with fabric and dope, and favourable results were recorded. This led to the concept of the solid leading edge, which extended each wing chord by six inches at the base and three inches at the wingtip – hence the wing's '6-3' nickname. The 51st FW had the opportunity to test the new fighter in combat in August 1952 when it sent three modified F-86Fs into 'MiG Alley'. The aircraft met with overwhelming approval from the pilots that flew them.

Thus orders were cut to immediately modify the F-86Fs that were already in-theatre. The new Sabres dramatically closed the high-speed performance gaps that existed between the F-86 and the MiG-15, boosting the American jet's top speed to 695 mph at sea level and 600 mph at 35,000 ft, and its maximum operating altitude up to 52,000 ft. The '6-3' wing also made the F-model considerably more manoeuvrable at those higher altitudes. Finally, the F-86F could also climb more rapidly thanks to its bigger J47-GE-27 engine, the jet being 16 mph faster and with a rate of climb some 300 ft per minute better than the F-86E.

One of the first pilots to reap the benefits associated with the F-86F was future ace 1Lt Hal Fischer, who joined the 39th FS in September 1952 with 109 missions in the F-80C already under his belt following a previous combat tour with the 8th FBG's 80th FBS. Fischer would claim ten kills with the jet in just four months, although this success was occasionally tempered by mechanical maladies;

'The F-86F was a very dependable machine, but on occasions its malfunctions scared the heck out of the pilot. On one of my very early missions a mechanical problem gave me a real scare. I was flying in the No 2 position on a morning mission. As we broke ground on take-off, I reduced power to keep from over running the leader and nothing happened. I moved out to the side, tuned my radio to another channel and reported to my flight lead that it was impossible for me to reduce power. I had no option but to keep climbing above the airfield, for in the event of an engine flame out I would be able to bail out safely. Flight lead had no advice to give me so I switched to the operations frequency, where the Ops officer told me that if I placed the fuel switch in the emergency position I would be able to manipulate the throttle.

'Easing on the fuel switch, the engine immediately reduced power and gave immediate indications of a flame out. It was a dicey situation to be in, but the rpm stabilised, and as long as I held the emergency fuel switch on, I could control the power. However, the fuel switch was above the throttle on the left side of the cockpit, and in order to adjust the power I had to hold the stick with my knee and use my right hand for the manipulation of the throttle! It was a little awkward to do this, but I managed to fly over an open area where I could drop my tanks before coming in to land. With great difficulty I finally managed to make a long low approach. On landing, I switched the throttle off completely and rolled into the revetment area and off the main runway.'

Fischer's experience was just one of the myriad emergencies that Sabre pilots endured either in a hostile area or over friendly territory close to their home base whilst flying combat-weary jets. When faced with such a serious mechanical failure, the experience level of the pilot had everything to do with saving a precious F-86 so that it could fight another day.

This photograph of ten-kill ace Capt Harold Fischer was taken on 31 March 1953, minutes after he had extricated himself from the cockpit of this F-86F after completing yet another 'MiG Alley' sweep. The 39th FS ace had claimed his tenth, and last, MiG-15 ten days earlier. Promoted to captain on 25 February 1953, Fischer came down over China one week after this shot was taken after claiming two MiG-15s destroyed. His F-86F-1 (51-2852) was almost certainly hit by debris from the second MiG. Neither of these kills were ever credited to Fischer because his gun camera film was lost along with his Sabre. The ace remained incarcerated in a Mukden prison until 31 May 1955 (*Earl Shutt*)

An ever-growing number of small 'specialty' shops cropped up right outside the main gate at Suwon during the 51st FW's time in-theatre. Enjoying a thriving trade, these businesses were well patronised by both wing personnel and support staff on base (*Carl Stewart*)

During the 30-month period that the Sabre was involved in combat missions in the Korean War, many younger, more inexperienced pilots forced to deal with similar in-flight emergencies were not as lucky as 1Lt Fischer, and they lost their lives and/or their aircraft.

Evidently, Fischer had more than his share of tense situations in the cockpit that did not involve MiG-15s. Here, he recalls another incident where he had an opportunity to fly a Sabre that needed to be delivered to Far East Material Command in Tokyo for overhaul;

'Right after my first MiG kill, I had a chance to ferry a disabled Sabre that required some major work. It had bellied in at Suwon, and when the groundcrew raised it with hydraulic jacks and lowered the gear, they determined that it was flyable and requested a ferry pilot to take it to Japan. The decision was made to send it to Far East Material Command in an effort to get it back into mission rotation rather than to use it as a source of spare parts. The groundcrew did not know the full extent of the damage to the Sabre, so it was limited to day flying under visual flight rules.

'The first indication I had that things were not right with this jet came on take-off, when I noticed that the airspeed indicated via the cockpit instrumentation was just 40 knots! My first thought was that the pitot cover was still in place, but I distinctly remembered removing it. There are two fears that all pilots have – an inadvertent gear-up landing and taking off with the pitot cover still on! Discovering in this case that it was only a faulty airspeed indicator, and realising the length of time it would take to burn off fuel before returning to base to have it repaired, I decided to press on toward Tsuiki AB, in Japan.

'If the weather was bad once I reached Tsuiki then the base would have to launch a jet and have it fly on my wing during my approach. That way I would be able to get my true airspeed from my wingman. Another factor I had to contend with was that the undercarriage doors had been removed, which meant that the jet would require a greater power setting than normal.

'I was able to land at Tsuiki without any further problems, and before I went to base ops to file a flight plan for Tokyo, I asked a crew chief to see if he could fix the airspeed indicator. The weather officer told me that there was a thick overcast in that area, but I should be able to break out at about 2000 ft. When I returned to the aircraft the crew chief informed me that he had been unable to make the repair, so I went ahead and took off.

'Despite a few problems brought about by the lack of fairings around the landing gear, I was able to maintain an altitude of 37,000 ft by applying 98 per cent power. As I approached Tokyo, sure enough, the entire area was covered in overcast. I reduced power, dropped the dive brakes and commenced the descent from bright sunlight into a thick murk. I could only monitor my rate of descent and the altitude to determine if everything was going okay, and after a while I broke out at 2000 ft just as I had been told. Now my problem was going to be landing at Tachikawa with its 5000-ft runway and high fences at both ends!

'This was one landing I wasn't going to attempt alone, so I contacted an F-80 that was flying locally from Johnson AB, which was close to Tachikawa. I explained to the pilot what my situation was, and that I needed to join up with him to determine my airspeed on landing approach. I took his left wing, and in a large circle to the left, we lined up to enter the traffic pattern at Tachikawa. He called out the airspeed as he dropped his gear and I followed suit, quickly followed by the flaps. Over the end of the runway, just over the high fence, I cut the power and the jet settled and touched down immediately. I was happy with the landing.

'I recalled an instructor during my early flight training who had covered up the airspeed indicator, thus allowing the student to judge the attitude of the aeroplane by the sound of the wind rushing between the wings and wires of the old biplane! It was just another day in the cockpit, and with the right amount of experience, it all turned out fine.'

KEEPING THEM FLYING

It was the hardworking groundcrews led by very capable crew chiefs that kept a high percentage of the Sabres in-theatre serviceable and ready to fight over 'MiG Alley' day in, day out. All the F-86 aces that survived the Korean War attributed their success in combat to their groundcrew, who provided them with an aircraft that was performing the way it should. And as with all previous aerial conflicts, the pilots were only 'borrowing' their Sabres, as these were actually 'owned' by the crew chief and his men.

One such crew chief was A/2C Earl L Shutt, who was responsible for a 39th FS F-86F that bore the names *MiG Master* and *Mighty Mouse*. Having endured numerous harrowing sorties over the Yalu, the Sabre was passed on to the Chinese Nationalist Air Force post-war. Here, A/2C Shutt reflects on 'his' F-86 from a crew chief's perspective;

Most of the heavy equipment needed to maintain the F-86s in-theatre at the various forward bases in South Korea was brought in aboard the USAF's cavernous C-124s. Here, groundcrew prepare to unload several Sabre engines at Suwon AB. The turnover of powerplants within the 51st FW was very high due to the sheer number of sorties being flown by the wing (*USAF*)

'Looking back to my tour with the 39th FS, I do not remember very many Sabres that returned from a combat mission with heavy battle damage. The ones I recall had holes in their wings and fuselage from cannon rounds shot at them by the MiGs. All of these were repairable, and they were back in the air in a short time. The only fighter I recall landing at Suwon in really bad shape was a Marine Corps F9F Panther. It was hit numerous times by ground fire, and its landing gear was not working. It slid down the runway, on fire, and when it finally came to a stop, the pilot got out okay. There was no way that that jet would fly again.

'Usually, when a pilot returned from a combat mission he would note on the flight record book any problems he may have encountered during the mission. Most of these were minor in nature and easy to correct. A major problem recorded by the pilot usually "Red-X'd" the jet, immediately grounding it until it had been fixed. One of the most frequent problems afflicting the F-86 was loss of cabin pressure. About 90 per cent of the pressure failures were caused by a faulty dump valve which was located behind the pilot's seat, and it was no problem to change out.

'The main responsibility of the crew chief was a rapid turn around time for his aircraft. It was always a challenge to see how fast you could get your jet ready for the next mission. This meant correcting any problems that had been written up by the pilot, installing a new set of external drop tanks (if the Sabre had encountered MiGs on the previous mission), refuelling the jet, checking to make sure that the armourers had reloaded all six machine guns and verifying that all of them were working properly.

'Once everything was ready, we would report to the flight chief. He would then indicate that your Sabre was ready to fly. Lists of "up" jets would then go to squadron operations, where pilots flying the next mission were assigned to a specific aircraft. Some of our F-86s would fly a morning mission and then be ready to go again in the afternoon. Although a certain pilot was assigned to an F-86, and he had his name on it, a number of other pilots got to fly it too, and many of the multiple kill symbols on the Sabres were not the result of one pilot's gunnery skills.'

Maj William Whisner's F-86E-10 51-2735 is readied for its next sortie by hardworking groundcrewmen from the 25th FS at Suwon in early 1952. Although Whisner finished his tour in Korea in mid-March 1952 with 5.5 victories to his credit, his Sabre was adorned with victory stars denoting his damaged claims (six) too (*Richard Immig*)

COUNTERING THE MiGs

American, British, South African and Australian aircraft bore the brunt of combat air tasking from land bases and aircraft carriers during the Korean War. And although they succeeded in keeping a numerically far superior force at bay for more than three years, they endured political restrictions throughout this time when it came to prosecuting the aerial war. Just as in World War 2, when fighters and bombers had to travel great distances to reach the heart of enemy territory, most targets of value in North Korea lay far beyond the frontline. But unlike the previous conflict, the Korean campaign was fought against the broader backdrop of the Cold War, which meant that it became the first of several conflicts effectively run by politicians rather than generals.

As a result of this political interference communist aircraft could seek sanctuary from UN fighters at airfields in nearby Manchuria, which could not be bombed because such attacks might have triggered a lethal nuclear war with China. This advantage allowed the fast-flying MiG-15s to employ a wide variety of tactics that the Sabre pilots were constantly striving to defeat.

Just north of the Yalu River were four major MiG airfields – Tapao, Antung, Tatungkou and Takishan. Within this complex were literally hundreds of new swept-wing fighters that were perfectly safe from the threat of aerial bombing.

It would have been easy for the F-86s to have flown cover for B-29 bombers (see *Osprey Combat Aircraft 29 - B-29 Superfortress Units of the Korean War* for further details) sent to destroy these sites should they have been given permission to attack them. However, they remained strictly off limits throughout the war, so the only way for the Sabre units to maintain aerial supremacy for the UN air forces was to keep the threat bottled up north of the Yalu. South of the river, in North Korea, were 34 airfields that were attacked by UN fighter-bombers. As quickly as communist groundcrews could make them operable, they would be hit again. Reconnaissance pilots tasked with keeping an eye on the operability of these bases stated that they spent so much time over them that they dreamed about the airfields at night!

The only two airfields that ever housed any MiG activity in North Korea were Sinuiju and Uiju, and then only for very brief periods.

Early F-86E-10 51-2732 of the 16th FS taxies out at the start of a mission from Suwon AB in 1952. Despite suffering heavy 37 mm cannon damage from a close encounter with a MiG-15 soon after this photograph was taken, 51-2732 survived the war and eventually ended up back in the US with the 170th FS in 1954 (*Iven Kincheloe*)

On some days, the airspace above 'MiG Alley' was a mass of swept-wing fighters, duelling one minute and then nothing in sight the next. Although the 'arena' for these deadly engagements was not overly long in length, it had great vertical depth that ranged from 50,000 ft down to tree-top height. The published dimensions of what has become known as 'MiG Alley' are stated as 6500 square miles, and if you factor in the depth, the overall area covered equates to 65,000 cubic miles.

In this vast fighting 'amphitheatre', the F-86 pilots were always at a disadvantage, for the enemy operated from air bases that were only a few miles away, and each of these provided a safe haven from attack. The MiG-15 could also reach higher service ceilings of 50,000+ ft, allowing pilots to choose the time and place for their clashes with the Sabres. Furthermore, the communists had perfected the art of ground control interception (GCI), allowing them to attack the F-86 formations at their weakest point. Yet despite all of these advantages, the Sabre squadrons in-theatre continued to achieve an outstanding kill ratio over the MiG-15.

With enemy fighter squadrons changing their tactics almost daily, it was hard for USAF pilots to prepare for what they might encounter when next they ventured over the Yalu. This general feeling of confusion was summed up in the following line taken from a combat report written by an unnamed 51st FW pilot in 1952. 'Tactics that are successful in the morning may be obsolete in the afternoon'!

Most of the tactics used by the communist pilots were designed to exploit the MiG-15's exceptional rate of climb, as well as the fighter's numerical advantage. By the end of 1952, intelligence sources had determined that there were more than 30 'manoeuvres' or tactics being used by these pilots. In reality, the only aircraft that these had a negative

Lt Col George Ruddell, CO of the 39th FS, pulls into his parking slot after a wild dogfight with MiG-15s on 17 April 1953 – notice the soot streaks around his gun ports. The veteran fighter pilot had just claimed his fourth MiG-15 kill, and had achieved ace status in the process, for he had scored two victories flying P-47Ds in the ETO in 1944. Ruddell would become the USAF's 31st jet ace on 18 May whilst at the controls of this very jet, F-86F-10 51-12940 (*Earl Shutt*)

A flight of four Sabres from the 16th FS heads south following a combat air patrol over North Korea. The jets have all dropped their external tanks, which indicates that they have been in close proximity to MiG-15s. However, the pilot of *PATRICIA ANN* has not had to resort to firing his guns (*Phil Hunt*)

Also seen on page 29, 51-2732 reveals the combat damage it received at the hands of a MiG-15 in late 1952. Although the communist jet was equipped with slow-firing 23 mm and 37 mm cannon, it only took one or two solid hits from either of these weapons to bring a Sabre down. This F-86E served as a sober reminder to 51st FW pilots that they were indeed vulnerable should they allow a MiG-15 to get in behind them. The holes in the right wing flap and air brake were caused by two 37 mm rounds (*Bill Nowadnick*)

effect on were the slower fighter-bombers, for the F-86 pilots usually developed a counter tactic to neutralise the 'manoeuvre' soon after it had first been encountered.

About five months into the 4th FW's deployment to Korea, MiG-15 pilots began using a tactic referred to as the 'Zoom and Sun'. This was a high-speed version of the hit-and-run attack used in World War 2, where the pilot took advantage of the sun's position.

This manoeuvre lingered well into the 51st FW's tenure, because the MiG-15 pilots always had the altitude advantage (48,000 ft to 50,000 ft) at the start of every engagement. The Sabre patrols would usually hit 'MiG Alley' at about 40,000 ft, flying at a high mach number. One of the 16th FS pilots stated that the only way to prevent this tactic from being deadly was to remain fully aware of what was above you – typically, one or more MiG-15s! The slow firing rate of the three cannon fitted in the nose of the communist jet gave the USAF pilot a small window of opportunity to get out of the way of the 'orange golf balls' whizzing past his canopy if he had spotted the attacking MiG in time.

As the enemy fighters came through the Sabre formations with blinding speed, it was difficult to drop the F-86's nose in time to allow the pilot to set off after the MiG-15s. As soon as the diving communist aircraft bottomed out after its diving attacking, the jet's greatest asset came into play – its ability to zoom back up onto its high-altitude 'perch'.

There was also another tactic that proved to be very dangerous to the Sabre pilots as it was difficult to spot in advance. A small number of the MiG-15s in-theatre were painted up in greenish-brown camouflage so as to allow them to blend in with the terrain below, and the pilots of these aircraft regularly performed the 'Uppercut' manoeuvre.

When employing this tactic, either an element of two MiGs or a flight of four would position themselves, with the help of their GCI, at between 20,000 ft and 25,000 ft in the path of an F-86 patrol. As the Sabres dove down for a firing pass, several more camouflaged MiGs would be laying in wait at low level ready to zoom up and ambush the attacking F-86s as they bottomed out of their dives. Usually, the Sabre pilots were totally focused on the enemy fighters they were attacking, leaving them vulnerable to attack from additional jets.

Ultimately, this tactic proved to be unsuccessful for the MiG squadrons, as all Sabre pilots soon became very wary of attacking pairs of communist fighters trolling around at the lower altitudes. However, in theory at least, it was a good tactic.

As previously mentioned, the MiG-15 pilots were constantly experimenting with new tactics and formations throughout 1952 following the introduction of the F-86E, and the enlarged Sabre force in-theatre. Senior flight leaders from both wings were quick to counter these manoeuvres following their reporting by pilots who had witnessed them

51st FW CO Col John Mitchell (right) congratulates Maj Clyde Wade soon after the latter had flown the wing's 25,000th sortie on 30 April 1953. This is the same Mitchell that led the famous 'Yamamoto Mission' on 18 April 1943, which resulted in the death of the architect of the Pearl Harbor raid. Having claimed 11 kills in World War 2 flying P-38s, P-39s and P-51s, Mitchell downed a further four MiG-15s (and damaged two more) whilst leading the 51st FW in 1953. Maj Wade was credited with a solitary MiG kill (*Clyde Wade*)

Gen Glenn O Barcus (left), commander of the Fifth Air Force, and 51st FW CO Col John Mitchell pose for a photograph in front of the 39th FS's operations hut. A fighter pilot in World War 2, Barcus had just returned from flying a mission with the squadron (*Dean Abbott*)

over 'MiG Alley'. And while new tactics were always treated with respect, the primary concern of most Sabre pilots was the ever increasing number of MiG-15s that they were having to face over the Yalu River.

AGGRESSIVE MiGS

In June 1952, Sabre units saw evidence that the communist air command had changed tactics yet again, abandoning its policy of high flying and stand-offish patrols. Suddenly, there had been a reduction in the number of MiG-15s visible at bases in Manchuria to UN reconnaissance assets flying missions at altitude just south of the Yalu. Only 298 fighters were sighted in the air over 'MiG Alley' that month, compared with twice this number in April.

The most noticeable change came in the various engagements fought by the F-86 pilots in June. The communist fighters had reacted aggressively to the Sabres' presence in 'MiG Alley', coming down and fighting with little hesitation. These jets were not being flown by beginners either, and three F-86s were lost in aerial combat during the month while 20 MiG-15s were claimed to have been destroyed.

June 1952 also marked the start of a nightfighter campaign by the MiG-15 force, communist units attempting to counter increased B-29 night attacks that were inflicting heavy damage to supply movements heading south across the Yalu River. Superfortresses had been forced to make nocturnal attacks from October 1951 onwards after losses suffered to MiG-15s in daylight raids had rendered these missions almost suicidal.

Despite facing overwhelming odds when going up against the MiG-15s, the 51st FW went into combat well prepared thanks to a cadre of experienced pilots that had been transferred in from the 4th FW to lead the wing. Expecting to be vastly outnumbered was commonplace for Sabre pilots, and a tactic that the new fighter pilots quickly learned from the 'old heads' of the 4th was to immediately turn into the attacking formation of MiGs regardless of how badly they were outnumbered. This always seemed to cause confusion among the communist pilots, and in many instances caused them to head back north and the safety of the Yalu.

Indeed, the only enemy pilots who seemed equipped to deal with this counterattacking tactic were the 'honcho' instructors, who usually operated in formations that were smaller in number than those typically associated with the MiG-15. These pilots would match skills and aggressiveness on an equal basis with their counterparts flying F-86s. However, when the MiG formations were extremely large, the 'honchos' usually tried to avoid getting caught up in the disorganised 'fur ball' fights synonymous with these engagements. When they wanted to fight, the instructors would venture south of the Yalu River with just a handful of their best students for company.

A World War 2 ace with 20.75 kills to his credit, Col Walker 'Bud' Mahurin joined the 51st FW in December 1951 and claimed 3.5 MiG-15 victories with the wing, prior to assuming command of the 4th FW in March 1952. One of the best Sabre pilots to see combat in Korea, Mahurin was a strong advocate of the F-86 as a fighter-bomber. He eventually fell victim to communist AAA whilst conducting a low-level attack on North Korean targets on 13 May 1952 and spent the rest of the war as a PoW in Manchuria. Mahurin is seen here on the 25th FS flightline in early 1952 (*Iven Kincheloe*)

F-86F-1 51-2895 *FRIVOLOUS FRAN* was flown by the 16th FS from late 1952. Bearing the name *SWEET JEANNE* on its port side, the jet survived the war and was transferred to the Chinese Nationalist Air Force (*Russ Knoebel*)

In debriefing reports, the MiG-15 pilots were put into two categories – 'honcho' and 'student'. Col John W Mitchell, who assumed command of the 51st FW from Col Gabreski on 13 June 1952, stated that when his wing intercepted MiGs, the 'students' gave his pilots an easy time of it and they usually scored some kills, but the 'honchos' posed a different challenge altogether. 'When we locked up with one of the instructor types, we knew immediately that our skills would be tested to the limit'.

While there were numerous tactics used by the MiG pilots, there were some innovative ones used by the Sabre 'drivers' too. Many of those concocted in early 1952 were far from perfect, however, because the F-86E was unable to achieve an altitude advantage over the MiG-15. For example, a manoeuvre such as 'Trolling', which was used to stunning effect by F-86F pilots such as Capt Joseph McConnell from the autumn of 1952 onwards, could not be performed in earlier versions of the Sabre due to them lacking the F-model's more powerful engine.

'Trolling' required a flight of F-86s to fly in the contrails whilst a second flight would be positioned above the 'cons' at between 45,000 ft and 50,000 ft. MiG pilots would track the 'cons' and set up for the attack, not realising that there were Sabres above the target jets just waiting to pounce.

Using tactics like the 'Yo-Yo' and 'End Run', MiG-15s were occasionally able to break through the F-86 fighter screen and get clean shots at the F-80s and F-84s. More often than not, however, enemy pilots failed to take advantage of this through a combination of over-eagerness, poor gunnery skills and general ineptness in the cockpit brought about by being thrown into combat before they had been properly trained. It has to be borne in mind here that very few of the MiG pilots in-theatre had any combat experience to fall back on, as did their World War 2-era 'honcho' instructors.

In August 1952, the communist fighter units stepped up the pace, and the overall number of MiG-15 kills credited to the Sabres doubled from 17 in July to 34. Still more clashes occurred in September, when 64 MiGs went down. Records kept by both wings indicated that their 36-jet flights were typically meeting groups of enemy fighters that numbered at least 50 aircraft in total. Although suffering from numerical inferiority, the USAF wings found that these odds were just about right, for it gave them room to manoeuvre when dogfighting, rather than having to deal with 100+ fighters at a time as had previously been the case. The larger formations

had drastically increased the possibility of mid-air collisions. The Sabre units took full advantage of these reduced odds, and only suffered losses of two or three aircraft per month between June and September.

However, in October the MiG formations reverted to their old ways, flying at altitudes well above the F-86 formations and very seldom choosing to come down and fight. This was reflected in the total kills for that month, which dropped back to 27. Four 51st FW Sabres were also lost during October, but none were actually listed as having been caused by direct contact with MiG-15s.

During this period some of the larger, high-flying, MiG formations penetrated as far south as Wonsan in early morning sweeps. These aircraft posed a serious threat to the fighter-bomber missions sortied soon after dawn, and they were immediately countered by sending up barrier patrols at first light to catch the MiGs in the act. In these cases, the 'fluid four' flights favoured by the F-86 wings were at a distinct disadvantage because of the sheer number of deep intruders facing them. To help redress this imbalance, the 51st FW began sending out flights of six jets rather than the standard four, whilst the 4th FW was sometimes known to launch eight Sabres in a flight on these missions. These barrier patrols did the job, as only one F-84 was lost prior to the intrusions stopping in late October.

Lt Lewis V Sykes flew Sabres with the 16th FS on the early morning patrols, and here he reflects on a mission involving a six-ship flight;

'In the autumn of 1952, the FEAF "brass" thought that it would be to our advantage to try flying formations that contained six F-86s rather than standard four, or two flights of eight. Thank goodness this idea was short-lived, as it was very difficult to maintain formation, especially when turns were made at altitude. I am sure they thought it would give us more aircraft in a given spot when we were attacked from above by the MiGs.

'On this one mission, we were just approaching a big dam up north at about 40,000 ft, with me in the No 5 slot, when I saw a "sun glint" above us at our "eleven o'clock" position. I called a turn in that direction, and sure enough, seconds later, two MiG-15s came diving down on us with their 23 mm and 37 mm cannon firing in our direction. There were floating red balls drifting all around us, but luckily none hit their mark!

'Almost immediately, their leader's aircraft, apparently having exceeded his mach, just quit flying and started tumbling through the air! His canopy flew off and the pilot ejected. As I began a turn to set up an attack on his wingman, my wingman yelled over the radio, "Look out! You've got one on your nose!" I rolled out and there was the ejected pilot, his 'chute fully open, trying to slip out of my way. We somehow missed each other and I lost sight of his wingman. Interestingly enough, at that altitude that day, the temperature was about 50 degrees below zero, and we didn't think they were equipped with oxygen. In any event, the pilot probably froze to death before he got down to a lower,

There were several reasons why the alert crew could be scrambled, but their primary purpose was to protect their base from a surprise attack by enemy aircraft. Fully kitted up, these 25th FS pilots are being carried out to the alert pad at Suwon to work their shift (*John Winters*)

warmer altitude, or at least that is what we were told in the debriefing after the mission. At least all six of our Sabres returned to Suwon safely.'

TWO YEARS OF JET COMBAT

The first week of November 1952 marked the second full year of jet combat in the Korean War. F-80s and F9Fs had initially fought the air-to-air fight with MiG-15s until F-86As had made it into theatre in December 1950. In the intervening two years, the enemy had failed miserably in its attempts to beat the Sabre in combat.

By the end of 1952 it was evident that the communists had very little intention of initiating air attacks against UN positions on the Main Line of Resistance or air bases in South Korea. The overall strength and capabilities of the US air armada in-theatre was just too overwhelming, and the enemy feared serious losses should it have mounted an attack on UN forces close to, or south of, the bomb line. Such losses would almost certainly have revealed the nationality of some of the men flying the MiGs in-theatre, so senior air commanders stuck to using northwest Korea as the ultimate training ground for all pilots in the communist bloc. The war also created opportunities for the trial of new tactics that were aimed at defeating the western world's best combat aircraft, as well as a stage for showcasing the performance of new communist types.

A perfect example of this occurred on 17 December 1952 when two new Soviet Il-28 bombers flew just north of and parallel to the Yalu River in full view of several flights of F-86s that were on a combat air patrol. They kept their distance, but they wanted to make sure that the Americans reported, in detail, what they observed.

Intelligence sources for the Air Force surmised that the communist training class that started in November 1952 had evidently reached the final stages of the curriculum because of a sudden upswing in the levels of aggressiveness being exhibited by the MiG pilots in January 1953. Nevertheless, most of the total sorties recorded (2248) for the month saw the communist pilots flying in long trains at very high altitudes. However, on 648 occasions they came down to fight, and pilots were reportedly using every manoeuvre in the book, as well as refusing to break off even when they had a chance to dart back across the Yalu.

According to most of the 51st FW pilots that were engaged in combat in January, their foes were some of the best MiG-15 pilots ever encountered in Korea. Flying distinctively marked jets with blue undersides and copper-coloured uppersurfaces, these pilots were all classified as 'honchos'. Years after the war had ended, it was discovered that these men were from an all-weather fighter regiment posted in from East Germany, which may

The 16th FS's 1Lt Cecil G Foster poses for a publicity photograph in his F-86E-10 51-2738 at Suwon soon after he had become the USAF's 23rd jet ace on 22 November 1952. All nine of his kills were scored while flying with this unit, and he finished the war as the 16th FS's ranking ace (*USAF*)

have included a number of ex-Luft-waffe pilots within its ranks. Never-theless, 39 MiGs were downed in January, with the 51st FW claiming 25 of them.

Aside from throwing their best pilots into the fray, the MiG units also made a concerted effort to test the response times of the Sabre wings in the first weeks of 1953. Communist fighters would pene-trate south of Chongchon, knowing full well that their presence would generate an immediate response from the F-86 pilots manning the alert jets at Kimpo and Suwon.

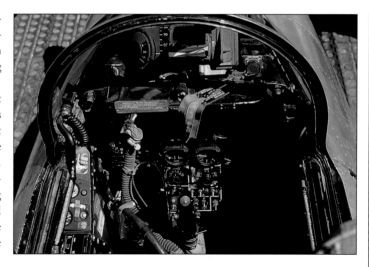

The cockpit of a MiG-killing F-86F of the 39th FS, photographed at Suwon in 1953 (*USAF*)

During February, the tactical air-control centre at Seoul detected MiG flights heading into this area on an almost daily basis, and as soon as the alert Sabres scrambled, the enemy jets turned around and headed back north. The sole purpose of this ploy was to probe UN radar defences and gauge response times, the information gained from these flights being passed on to bases throughout the Warsaw Pact, as well as Soviet airfields closer to Japan and Alaska. Such incursions continued into the 1980s, USAF air defences in northern Japan bearing the brunt of these sorties.

The F-86's fuel consumption was another aspect studied by the Soviets as they tried to develop tactics that would catch the American fighters at their most vulnerable point when low on 'gas'. The end result was the 'Box-In' tactic, which allowed enemy pilots to exploit the F-86s' low fuel state when the jets departed 'MiG Alley'. The 51st FW was the victim of this manoeuvre on numerous occasions, large formations of MiG-15s positioning themselves north of the Yalu just as its Sabres were ending their patrols south of the river. When the lead F-86 pilot called 'Bingo' over the radio and the formation turned south, their communist counterparts knew that the USAF jets were now low on fuel.

At that time, the MiGs would cross the river at high speed and pursue the F-86s south. Twenty minutes prior to this, a larger group of enemy fighters would have made a wide, sweeping turn out of view of the Sabres south of Chongchon. With good radio contact with the trailing MiGs and their own GCI, the Chongchon group would then turn north in order to make a series of head-on passes against the retiring, and vul-nerable, F-86s. Fortunately, much-improved coverage by US radar sites usually alerted the retiring Sabre pilots to the ploy, and this allowed them to avoid numerous ambushes.

However, as a result of these late-mission dogfights, many of the F-86s involved did not have enough

The key to the Sabre's success in a dogfight was to make sure that the fighter's relatively lightweight 0.50-cal rounds converged on the target at exactly the same point as the pilot was seeing through his gunsight. Thus, all F-86s spent time getting their weapons boresighted by hardworking groundcrews. This crude shelter, hastily erected from empty packing crates, protected the cockpit and personnel from the harsh winter weather whilst jets were being boresighted at Suwon (*Robert Mount*)

This historic image was taken by a 51st FW photographer on the afternoon of 24 January 1953. To the left of the shot is Capt Dolph Overton, who had claimed his fifth, and last, kill that very morning to become the USAF's 24th jet ace. Sat in the cockpit of the F-86 is Capt Harold Fischer of the 39th FS, who had just returned from a mission in which he too had downed his fifth MiG-15 – a victory which made him the Air Force's 25th jet ace. On the right is Capt Cecil Foster (the USAF's 23rd jet ace) of the 16th FS, who had scored two kills that same day (*Cecil Foster*)

Specialists work on the radar gunsight of 25th FS F-86E-10 51-2735 in a revetment at Suwon in the spring of 1953. This aircraft subsequently served with the 35th FW post-war (*Bill Nowadnick*)

fuel left to return to their bases, forcing pilots to eject over or close to UN-held Cho-do Island, off Korea's west coast. In an attempt to counter this tactic, the F-86 wings started sending up several Sabre screens, guided by the radar sites, to protect the returning flights. With ample fuel, these fighters were able to break up the 'Box-In' formations.

When the final score came in for February 1953, the 4th FW had made the most of its increased opportunities to claim 26 kills to the 51st's seven. Three F-86s were lost to MiGs – two 4th FW jets and one from the 51st.

Behind these monthly kill statistics, great rivalry existed between the two wings when it came to boasting the leading ace in-theatre. The USAF's first jet ace, Maj James Jabara (with six kills from 1951), had returned to Korea for a second tour with the 4th FW on 12 January 1953. He quickly hit his straps, and along with Capt 'Pete' Fernandez and Col Royal Baker, the trio went head-to-head within the 4th FW in early 1953 as they chased the coveted 'aces of aces' crown. For the 51st FW, the leading contenders were Capts Joe McConnell and Hal Fischer.

The media also picked up on this 'ace race', thus garnering publicity back at home for the main contenders in Korea. By April 1953 the race had narrowed somewhat, but the intensity had grown. May proved to be the pivotal month in determining the highest scoring ace, with Capt Fernandez breaking out from his rivals by boosting his tally to 14.5 kills on the 16th. His lead did not last long, however, for Capt McConnell replied with six kills between 13 and 18 May, taking his final tally to 16.

The publicity created by the 'ace race' finally caught up with the leading Sabre pilots in-theatre when senior officers in the FEAF discovered that McConnell had flown 106 missions and Fernandez a whopping 125! The stipulated tour length was 100 missions, so both pilots were immediately grounded by the Fifth Air Force and sent home. This left Maj James Jabara to finish things off, and although he came on strong in June with five kills, and then claimed another on 15 July, he ended his second combat tour with a combined total of 15 victories.

Having fought the MiG-15 for more than two years, the US military had still to get its hands on a fully working example of the jet – conversely, the communist had gotten hold of several force-landed examples of the Sabre. In the final stages of the Korean War, a secret operation was hatched by US Intelligence that would hopefully result in a MiG-15 being delivered to them intact. Codenamed Operation *Moolah*, official

records reveal that planning for the event had ended in March 1953. Approved by the UN Joint Psychological Warfare committee on 1 April, *Moolah* was to be carried out later that month. The plan was simple enough – the Americans would offer $50,000 to any communist pilot that flew his MiG-15 to a friendly airfield in South Korea. An additional $50,000 was offered to the first pilot to do so. News of the plan would be spread in the form of leaflets distributed by nightflying B-29s.

16th FS pilot 2Lt Leland W Carter recalls more of the details, and how *Moolah* affected the F-86 pilots at Suwon;

'We were called into a big meeting at Suwon involving every pilot in the 51st FW. The "top brass" from Tokyo then came in to brief us on the fact that they were going to drop leaflets offering any pilot that would defect in his MiG a lot of money, tax free! We were also briefed on the fact that the instructions on the leaflet stated that said MiG pilot would approach our airspace with wheels and flaps down. We were told not to shoot at any MiG flying south that fitted this description. As far as I remember, none of the MiG pilots took them up on the offer. After our meeting, B-29s flew over the bases in and around Antung dropping thousands of leaflets.

Strangely enough, for the next few days after the drop no MiGs flew. Evidently, if there were any mercenaries or pilots not truly dedicated to the cause within their ranks, they were not taking a chance that one would flee. I do recall that a pilot defected after the war had ended.'

ENDLESS ENCOUNTERS

June 1953 proved to be the record breaker for the F-86 in Korea, both in terms of the number of MiGs destroyed and Sabres lost in combat. No fewer than 78 MiG-15s were claimed to have been downed, but at a cost of 23 Sabres (14 of the latter were lost to enemy fighters and the remainder to operational causes). Unusual weather conditions in northwest Korea during the month also played their part in the ferocious battles fought out in 'MiG Alley'.

Normally, most engagements between F-86s and MiG-15s were initiated by the latter due the communist fighters' altitude advantage.

Three F-86Es in a flight of four 16th FS jets fly at extreme altitude over North Korea in the autumn of 1952. With their external tanks jettisoned, these aircraft had evidently been approached by MiG-15s, but with no powder residue on their gun ports, the American pilots never got within range to open fire on the communist fighters. The jet in the foreground was amongst the first Sabres issued to the 51st FW in-theatre, and it is seen here adorned with a row of seven victory stars below its cockpit. The aircraft was lost in an operational accident on 10 May 1953 whilst still assigned to the 16th FS. Having flown with both the 25th and 16th FSs, F-86E-10 51-2737 survived the war and was eventually salvaged in the US in the mid 1950s, while Canadair-built F-86E-6 52-2842 was written off on 6 October 1952 (*USAF*)

However, for much of June 1953 the general area around the Yalu River was covered with high-level cloud, which forced the MiG pilots to come down well below 40,000 ft. They may have also thought that the limited visibility would adversely affect the F-86s' ability to defend the fighter-bombers hitting targets in northwestern Korea. With the MiGs coming south at lower altitudes, aggressive Sabre pilots initiated 70 of the 92 engagements in June – this translated into more kills for the F-86s.

In the statistics for the month, there was also credit given to both wings for a total of 11 probables and 41 damaged. The biggest day for the F-86 pilots was on 30 June, when they downed 16 jets to break the previous record of 13 kills, which had been matched three times in the war.

After almost 30 months of jet combat, on 22 July 1953, a relatively new 2nd Lieutenant called Sam P Young from the 25th FS was part of a MiG sweep over the Yalu River. During his previous missions as an element wingman, he had not had a chance to actually engage an enemy fighter. This particular mission was flown just before dusk in an effort to catch some late flights of MiG-15s south of the river. Suddenly, four enemy jets cut across below Young's formation, presenting him with his chance for a kill. Reacting instinctively, he pounced on one of the MiGs and opened fire with all six of his 0.50-cal machine guns. Seconds later, Young was credited with a kill, but this was not the end of the story.

This victory was officially credited as the 800th MiG-15 to be shot down over Korea, and it ended up being the final MiG kill of the war.

When the ceasefire came into effect five days later, there had been a lull in MiG activity since 2Lt Young made his kill five days previously. In the 72 hours immediately after the 800th kill, the weather had been too bad to fly, and most fighters on both sides remained sat on the ground. On the last day of the war both the Sabres and the MiG-15s were up, but neither side penetrated the boundaries of the Yalu. The communist pilots knew that the end of the conflict was just hours away, so they chose not to mix it up.

There were at least two 51st FW Sabres that were adorned with experimental paint schemes on their vertical stabilisers during the wing's time in Korea. F-86F-10 51-2941 featured smaller black and white checkers on its tail for a short period of time, as did 51-2864. Subsequently transferred to the 4th FW's 335th FS, 51-2941 survived the war and was eventually amongst the 320 F-86Fs passed on to the Chinese Nationalist Air Force from 1954 onwards (*Gil Lowder*)

Pilots from the 25th FS gather on the flightline to pose for a squadron photograph in the spring of 1953. Marked up with red command stripes on its nose, the CO's Sabre provides the backdrop for the shot (*John Winters*)

FLYING WITH THE ACES

F or a handful of Sabre pilots, the gap between scoring their fourth and all-important fifth kills was both lengthy and nerve racking. The intense desire to achieve ace status is engrained in every fighter pilot as he goes through the rigours of learning to fly his aircraft competently. Once this phase in his career has been completed, the chances of him becoming an ace depend on his natural skills as a pilot, and luck (being in the right place at the right time).

For 1Lt Cecil G Foster, the opportunity to bridge the gap and 'make ace' came relatively quickly. Between 7 September and 22 October 1952 he claimed four MiG-15s destroyed and one damaged. However, for the better part of the next month Foster's missions were hampered by a combination of bad weather and a two-week spell of rest & recreation in Japan. Within 24 hours of returning to operational status on 21 November, he had been presented with the opportunity to claim his fifth kill and he took full advantage of it. Here, Foster describes the mission;

'We were required to escort an RF-80 on a photo-reconnaissance flight over MiG territory. I was named the mission leader, and I had to figure out how to coordinate the various Sabre flights that would be   covering the recce jet. My flight followed the RF-80 into the air, while the other flights assigned to the mission had already headed north.

'In order provide effective fighter protection for the unarmed recce jet, we had to maintain position by crossing back and forth, or by decreasing our airspeed. Once we crossed the bomb line, I radioed for the guys to check their guns and assume the combat spread position. We continued north for the recce bird's objective, which was the Sui-ho Dam. At the point where our external tanks ran dry, I told everyone to jettison them. All of the tanks fell free except for those attached to my aircraft – both of my tanks hung, which was very unusual.

'The alternate mission commander was a newly-assigned colonel that needed a little more experience in the area, although he was still a very capable pilot. He took over and my wingman and I pulled out of the formation. For the next few minutes, I made every effort to shake the tanks off the pylons. Nothing worked, so my wingman ,1Lt Ed Hepner, and I headed back toward Suwon.

'In the meantime, I kept trying to get rid of the tanks. Finally, I pulled out the circuit breaker that activated the tank release and left it out,

1Lt Cecil Foster returns to the 16th FS flightline at Suwon on the afternoon of 22 November 1952 after having just downed his fifth MiG-15 to 'make ace' (*Phil Hunt*)

1Lt Cecil Foster poses alongside his F-86E-10 51-2738 *THREE KINGS*, which he regularly flew while serving with the 16th FS in 1952-53. This photograph was taken in late September 1952 after he had claimed his second and third kills on the 26th of that month. Completing 98 missions and 161 combat hours whilst in-theatre, the nine-kill ace subsequently led the F-4 Phantom II-equipped 390th TFS in Vietnam in 1968-69, flying a further 165 missions and 325 combat hours (*Cecil Foster*)

before pushing it back in again. Then I punched the tank release button, located on the stick, and "boom", both tanks left the jet. Now that my tanks were gone we were ready to return to the mission.

'I radioed ahead and informed the mission leader that I was headed back to join them. He replied that they were too far ahead, and it would be too difficult for me to catch them up as they had to remain close to the photo-ship. I decided to join them as they exited the area instead. In the meantime, we were flying north toward the dam, listening to the radio chatter from the counter-air Sabres that were with the RF-80. They were over the target area and had just finished the mission, and were now in the process of turning back south.

'At that time, 1Lt Hepner and I spotted a flight of four MiG-15s just as we were about to meet head-on. All four of them fired at us, but we didn't get hit. I initiated a climbing turn, using what I called a "whiffleball" manoeuvre, which saw us climb, turn and then descend into a position to the left of the enemy flight. They made a hard right climbing turn, which put us almost in a scissors position, but in a crossing pattern. Due to my exuberance, I performed a loose barrel roll, which allowed us to maintain airspeed but lose forward position. However, I was able to get in behind the last two MiGs in the flight – not exactly in their "six o'clock", but a little off to one side. This close proximity then evolved into typical air-to-air manoeuvring (climbing, diving, pulling hard, rolling etc.).'

Both Foster and the MiG-15 pilots fired off a number bursts at one another, but neither was hit. He could tell by the way his adversary was flying that he was no amateur, and neither was the No 2 pilot in the element. Both were willing to stay in close and mix it with the F-86 pilots, with no indication that they wanted to break contact and race back north to the safety of Manchuria.

The entire time this fight was unfolding, Foster was listening to the radio chatter of the F-86 pilots that were watching over the RF-80. He could tell that they were well on their way back to Suwon, and probably out of danger from any MiG attacks. Happy that the primary mission objective had been achieved, he told Hepner that it was time to exit the area because their fuel was getting low. Both Sabre pilots made a sharp turn to the south at maximum speed. Looking back, they saw that the two MiGs were following them, closing from their 'six o'clock'!

When the enemy fighter behind Hepner had got within 2000 ft, Foster told him to break left while he broke right, and this manoeuvre put them in position to cover each others' tail. Seconds later, one of the MiGs scored hits on Hepner's jet with its cannon rounds. The situation was now critical, as both MiGs were still close and one F-86 was crippled;

'The MiG that was on Hepner's tail had seen me crossing over, and he broke off and flew straight ahead. As he did, I was able to execute a roll to

Pilots from the 51st FW have emerged from their mission briefing and are now strapping into their jets for a wing-strength effort up north. When all three squadrons were tasked to launch at the same time, this usually meant that the fighter-bombers were going to be out in large numbers, bombing targets just south of the Yalu River. Such missions greatly increased the Sabre pilots' chances of fighting MiGs (*Carl Stewart*)

the right and get back around behind and underneath him. At this time I lined him up and gave him a burst, with my aim being directed by my tracer rounds.

'On my third burst, I could see that I was scoring some major hits, and suddenly the MiG seemed to stop in mid-air. I was rapidly overrunning him, so I popped my speed brakes out, pulled my power back to idle and came up very close behind him and fired another burst. I knew my rounds were finding their mark, but I did not see any smoke or flames. The pilot did not seem to be reacting like he should have if his aircraft was getting raked with 0.50-cal rounds. His airspeed had dropped down to where he seemed to be standing still. Once again, my closure was too fast and it seemed like I was up his tailpipe. I pushed my nose down and went underneath him.'

Foster quickly realised that his closure rate would have him pass the MiG and leave him vulnerable directly in front of the enemy fighter, so he made a hard right followed by a hard left turn. As he went into the left turn, he looked up just as the MiG pilot ejected. It had been an important kill for Foster, but his troubles were not over yet. He had to find out where 1Lt Hepner was, for he was not answering his radio.

Minutes later, Foster received a call from his wingman stating that his instrument panel had been shot out and his canopy was gone. This made it impossible for him to hear any transmissions because of the wind noise. Hepner stated he was headed for Cho-do Island and he would eject there. After Foster heard the response from the helicopter rescue unit that they had him in sight as he ejected over the island, he knew that his wingman was in good hands. With his fuel critically low, Foster headed for Suwon and made it back with his Sabre literally flying on fumes.

He recalled that when he climbed out of the cockpit, he was soaking wet and shaking like a leaf. It had been the most traumatic experience of his combat career to date. This mission had put 1Lt Cecil G Foster in the record books as the USAF's 23rd jet ace of the war.

ROUTINE MISSIONS

The operational records of both Sabre wings in Korea were mostly filled with routine missions whose objectives were clearly defined – fly north to engage the MiGs and protect UN aircraft that might be in danger as they carried out their mission. What makes these records so interesting is the personal input from pilots that flew the missions and fought the MiGs.

Although there were many dogfights fought over the Yalu River during the 30 months that Sabres sparred with MiG-15s for aerial supremacy, very few of these clashes were dull, and each one had its own personality.

As previously mentioned, the 39th FS's Capt Joseph McConnell was the leading MiG killer of the Korean War with 16 victories, and his total bested the 4th FW's ranking ace by just one kill. Although there were only 39 US pilots classed as jet aces by war's end, many others came very close. Like the aces, these men possessed the same levels of skill, aggressiveness and situational awareness, but they did not enjoy the same luck as the select 39. They were simply not in the right place at the right time.

The new pilots that rotated into the 51st FW fresh from flying schools in the US were eager to 'shoot it out' with their communist counterparts, but it would be many months before they would get a crack at the enemy. Working up to element or flight lead (the shooters) was a slow process, and there were very few instances where new pilots were rushed into positions of importance. Typically, a tyro aviator would first be checked out in the F-86 in the locale near to Suwon, and after he had survived several familiarisation flights 'down south', he was deemed ready to experience combat, but only as a wingman.

1Lt Dean Abbott was one of those highly motivated pilots that ended up in the 39th FS. This was the same unit that double aces Hal Fischer and Joe 'Mac' McConnell served in, and Abbott possessed the necessary skills to fly as wingman for the latter pilot on numerous missions;

'I was very fortunate to fly some memorable missions with 'Mac'. On one of them, we were conserving fuel while working a combat air patrol over Cho-do Island. We were acting as spares to cover any one of 40+ Sabres that were patrolling over "MiG Alley" in the hope of luring a few up to fight. We would be able to cover any of them should they get into trouble. However, there was no action, and the Sabre formation headed for home. In the meantime, "Mac's" main hydraulic system had failed and he was forced to use the alternate system. The F-86 Dash-1 manual called for an immediate landing following such a failure, but that was not to be. Suddenly, the operators of the Cho-do radar facility called out MiG flights over Mukden, which was a large air base 80 miles into Manchuria.'

'Without a word, "Mac" turned north and we headed straight for Mukden! By the time we arrived, all of the MiGs had landed, so we made a lazy, time-consuming, 360-degree orbit above the base. I was doing my best to hold my breath, and we finished one circle without anything happening. I breathed a sigh of relief in the hope that we would head south, but that was not to be as "Mac" called for another orbit, which took several minutes. Once again nothing happened. Then we started heading back to Suwon, with just enough fuel to make it.'

These actions were typical of the confidence and daring associated with the Sabre pilots in Korea. McConnell had openly challenged the MiG pilots over their own base and they had refused to fight. There were also numerous incidents involving elements of Sabres that had flown far to the north of

Fitted with mandatory long range tanks, a pair of F-86Fs from the 39th FS taxi out at the start of a combat air patrol that will take them over 'MiG Alley'. The jet in the foreground is F-86F-1 51-2869, assigned to the 16th FS. Seen here undergoing a routine engine change, the fighter later served with the Chinese Nationalist Air Force post-war (*Carl Stewart*)

Antung, before racing back south at full throttle just above the enemy's runway. Many of these jets were fired at, but on other occasions their bold overflights were ignored. Such actions were not restricted to the 51st FW.

1Lt Abbott continues;

'My most memorable flight with McConnell occurred on 18 May 1953. By then he had already registered 13 kills. On this mission, we were trying to counter the MiG tactic of flying long trains of two-ship flights, one

behind the other. We had occasionally used the six-ship flights, but they proved to be too unwieldy. However, on this morning "Mac" was leading just such a flight. It didn't last long, as the No 5 Sabre aborted the take-off roll and No 6 remained behind with him. Now we were back to four. When we sighted MiGs in the far distance, No 3 could not get both of his tanks off, so he headed for home with his wingman. Now we were down to just "Mac" and I. We continued north to the Yalu.

'As soon as we arrived over the river, two MiGs flew over us, heading north. We turned after them and followed them across the Yalu into Manchuria. They were about half-a-mile in front of us, slightly high, and they knew we were behind them. Frequently dipping their wings to keep us in sight, there was no doubt in our minds that they were calling for help. We were not gaining on them, and it surprised me when "Mac" pulled his nose up, which resulted in a loss of airspeed – he was firing off a short burst in an attempt to slow his MiG down. If you hit them in the tail, their landing gear would often drop, making them a sitting duck.

'To my amazement, "Mac" scored some hits and the MiG lit up from strikes on its tail. I tried to do the same thing, shooting off quick bursts at the one I was behind, but I did not observe any hits.

The 51st FW's two top ranking aces discuss tactics prior to flying a combat air patrol over 'MiG Alley' in early 1953. On the left is Capt Joe McConnell and on the right is Capt Harold Fischer. Both men flew with the 39th FS during their combat tours. Behind them is McConnell's F-86F-15 51-12971 BEAUTIOUS BUTCH, which the ace was forced to abandon when it was struck by cannon fire from a MiG-15 moments after he had claimed his eighth kill on 12 April 1953 (Earl Shutt)

F-86E-10 51-2788 SNUFFY SMITH was assigned to the 16th FS in 1952-53. Note the multiple kill symbols painted beneath its windscreen. These were almost certainly scored by several different pilots, as the jet saw 18+ months of combat flying. It was flown by the Japan-based 35th FW post-war (USAF)

Boasting a replacement dive brake, veteran F-86E-1 50-598 was one of the very first Sabres assigned to the 16th FS in late 1951. Bearing the name *KAREN ANN* on the right side of its forward fuselage and *MY BEST BETT* on the left, this aircraft was flown by 1Lt Bernard Vise in 1952-53 (*Richard Thompson*)

'At that very moment the help started arriving, and I called out two flights of four MiG-15s approaching from "three o'clock" and "nine o'clock". I also spotted several others headed in our direction too. We broke hard into the closest flight, as they were much better targets than the original two jets. I inadvertently got out in front of one of them and he started firing at me. "Mac" rolled in behind him and shot him off my tail, the pilot immediately ejecting. We broke hard right again, and the same thing happened with me out in front. Another MiG came in behind me and started firing, while "Mac" did a half-roll and got in behind him. Seconds later the MiG was history.

'At some point during the action I remember calling out that there must be 30 MiGs nearby, to which "Mac" responded, "Yeah, and we've got them all to ourselves"! His exploits during this sortie made him the first triple ace of the war. For the next few minutes all we could do was break left and right in defensive mode. I am certain that the only reason we were not shot down is the fact that there were so many of them that they got in each others' way. We finally worked our way to the Yalu, and thankfully none of the MiGs followed us. We were so low on fuel that when we touched down at Suwon both of us were flying on fumes!'

HEIGHT ADVANTAGE

When Sabre pilots went up against MiG-15s, they knew that the biggest advantage the enemy had was his ability to get above them. This meant that a fatal attack could come out of the sun at any time, and they all hoped that when this happened, their opponent was a poor shot! The F-86 pilots did have one thing on their side to help them see the enemy before they could set up a firing run, however – the tell-tale contrails that all aircraft produce when flying at higher altitudes.

A group of 16th FS pilots gather outside the squadron's ops hut at Suwon to have their picture taken in late 1952. Standing at the extreme left is future ace Capt Dolph Overton. He became the USAF's 24th jet ace when he claimed five MiG-15s destroyed between 21 and 24 January 1953. Overton had previously completed a 100-mission tour in F-84 Thunderjets with the 49th FBG, prior to transitioning to F-86s at Suwon in August 1952 (*Phil Hunt*)

Each pilot flying north started looking for contrails about the time they were passing over Pyongyang. Many 51st FW veterans stated that one of the most memorable sights they remember from these missions was seeing the countless contrails from huge formations of MiG-15s cruising along at 50,000 ft. As previously mentioned, it was subsequently learned that these jets were usually being piloted by advanced students flying in trail over 'MiG Alley', safe in the knowledge that they could not be intercepted by F-86s at these rarefied altitudes. Most of the times, these large gag-

There were several factors that made the F-86 the dominant fighter in the Korean War, and one of them was its six rapid-firing 0.50-calibre machine guns. Although packing less of a punch than the MiG-15's three cannon, the Browning guns fired far more rapidly and were less prone to jamming. This photograph clearly reveals the positioning of the trio of weapons housed in the port gun bay (*Frank Harkins*)

gles never broke off and came down to fight. However, there were many occasions when their instructors took up the challenge, and most of these pilots were good adversaries.

Here, future ace 1Lt Cecil G Foster recalls the mission when he made his only double kill (he finished his tour with nine kills). This occurred on 26 September 1952, when the 16th FS was flying combat air patrols over 'MiG Alley' in an effort to lure the enemy up for a fight. Foster was element lead in a flight of four led by a Capt Bart;

'We flew to the mouth of the Yalu and turned east-northeast, staying just south of the river at 35,000 ft, with the sun at our backs. We kept a sharp eye out for contrails, and at that time there were none in our vicinity, but there were quite a few far to the north. Suddenly, my wingman spotted two MiGs ahead of us, crossing from left to right and slightly below. We dropped our tanks and began a descending hard right turn toward their stern position.

'My flight lead's dive was forcing us out of a good protective situation, so I began a climbing left turn which I intended to follow with a rapid reversal to put us in a position to cover Capt Bart. As soon as I started my climb, I was surprised to see six pairs of white puffs of smoke, which I first called as flak. I then realised that the puffs were caused by the MiGs dropping their external fuel tanks as we crossed right through their formation. I saw them flying in trail, each with a wingman close behind. At that time I made a hard reversal to the right.

'The MiG flight leader was in a hard left turn, and we entered a scissors manoeuvre, cutting across each others' nose. Their leader fired at us much too early, making a bad shot. I rolled level and called my wingman, informing him that I was in a scissors with six MiGs and could use a little help! As I called, I fired a one-second burst with my six 0.50-cal machine guns. I watched my tracers fly toward the MiG in what seemed like slow motion as I heard Capt Bart acknowledge my call for help. My tracers passed just aft of the lead MiG's tail and my bullets subsequently stitched a row of hits along the fuselage of his wingman.

'At that same instant, the lead MiG exploded in a large black and orange fireball. I yelled over the radio, "The MiG exploded, and the number two is burning!" The wingman's jet was trailing brown and black smoke as I pulled up sharply to miss the remaining MiGs as they flew past. If they fired at us, we didn't notice it, and they didn't score any hits.

'I kept my eyes on the second MiG, for it appeared to stop in the air, and my nose climbed to almost a vertical attitude. I continued with a rolling pullover and entered a nearly vertical dive as I followed the crippled fighter, which was now in an inverted position. One more quick burst and I realised that I was about to have a mid-air collision. I rotated my aircraft a quarter turn counterclockwise as my right wing passed between the MiG's wing and fuselage. This close call aged me ten years!

'I executed an immediate pull up and hard turn back into the damaged MiG that was falling like a leaf, still inverted. Two seconds later I saw the pilot floating below me in his parachute and a long red streamer dropping nearby. Later, I wondered why he had opened his 'chute at 35,000 ft – maybe he had forgotten to disconnect his low altitude ejection lanyard.

'I then called out to my wingman to make sure he was still with me. He answered quickly, and had managed to protect my back during the entire melee. We then flew towards the descending pilot so I could take pictures with my gun camera. I switched the firing controls to "safe", but did not get a picture because I had passed directly over the top of the parachute. The MiG pilot was frantically waving his arms, so he was either afraid that I was going to shoot him or he was struggling to connect his oxygen bottle. I seriously doubt if he survived the bail-out because of the high altitude he was at when he punched out.'

RENEWED OFFENSIVE

Despite the Armistice talks – held in May 1953 – hinting that the war may be coming to an end, the Chinese Army was still trying to mount a sizeable ground offensive that would drive the frontlines farther south, thus giving North Korea more territory than it had when the conflict started. UN air power had done its job well, however, preventing the stockpiling of supplies and equipment to support such an attack.

MiG activity over northwest Korea had also remained high, FEAF records showing that 60 communist jets had been shot down in May and 75 in June. These wild dogfights provided many wingmen with memorable missions to talk about. One such pilot was 2Lt Reginald W Adams Jr, who reached the 39th FS at Suwon in the final weeks of the war. He flew regularly with his CO, eight-kill ace Lt Col George I Ruddell;

'It was a beautiful flying day over North Korea, with unlimited visibility as my squadron launched a fully blown Yalu sweep – the wing sortied no fewer than 48 Sabres from the 16th, 25th and 39th FSs. There was also a big formation of fighter-bombers that were hitting targets well within MiG range, so we launched first so as to get into a position to stay between them and the enemy jets.

'I was flying wing for 1Lt Wade Kilbride in a flight of four jets that had Lt Col Ruddell as the flight lead. We were designated "Cobra" Flight. Flying with the boss was going to be tough, as he was aggressive, and you had to stay in close with him. He only had one power setting in his F-86F, and that was "full throttle" from the minute he took off to when he landed!

'Our sole tasking on this mission was to protect the F-84s and F-86F fighter-bombers as they carried out their air-to-ground mission.

'It did not take long for the action to start, as we observed six MiGs

The 16th FS erected a more permanent structure, complete with painted bombs and an entrance awning, to serve as its operations building in 1953. Elsewhere at Suwon, each of the 51st FW's Sabres had its own safe shelter and high sandbagged revetment (*Carl Stewart*)

F-86F-1 51-2905 *"JEAN'S JOY"* was assigned to the 39th FS in 1952-53. The kill symbols painted on the fuselage indicate that it had seen a lot of action. Despite this, the fighter survived the war and eventually saw service with the Chinese Nationalist Air Force on Formosa (*USAF*)

This photograph provides a close-up view of Lt Col George Ruddell's F-86F-10 *MIG MAD MAVIS* soon after he had returned to Suwon on 18 May 1953 with his fifth MiG kill. The 39th FS CO used up all of his ammunition on this particular mission (*Harold Chitwood*)

trying to sneak through our screen at very low altitude. Lt Col Ruddell immediately began a dive, which put us right on top of, and behind, their formation. He and his wingman took on the lead MiG and Kilbride set his sights on the leader of the second group. The other two MiGs broke their formation and disappeared. Although we lost sight of our flight lead, he eventually downed the MiG that he was after.

'Kilbride became engaged in a tight turn with his MiG, firing continuously and scoring numerous hits, while I observed and attempted to stay in the wing position to protect his tail. Thank God for the G-suit, as I was holding a constant 4 Gs to stay inside the turn. During the course of the action, the MiG pilot's wingman appeared on my left, attempting to get in position to fire on my leader. As the MiG pulled up on my left, I held my G-forces until I felt that it was time for me to do something to prevent his firing on Kilbride. I relaxed just enough stick pressure to put me in position to fire.

'My 0.50-cal tracers laced right through the canopy of the MiG, which immediately did a lazy roll over and headed for the ground. In spite of my gun camera film confirming the hits, I did not get any type of explosion. I suspect that I may have killed the pilot, as my tracers penetrated from the side where the MiG had very little armoured protection. Nevertheless, 51st FW Intelligence would not confirm a kill for me. I have often wondered since that day should I have broken off and followed the MiG down to confirm the kill. Needless to say, as a wingman, I was committed to staying with my leader, and to protect his "six o'clock".

'Shortly after my MiG-15 had gone down, Kilbride ran out of ammunition so he called me to continue the engagement – I pulled in behind the MiG he had been firing on. The enemy pilot evidently thought that the engagement was over, for he rolled out straight and level and then headed for the safety of the Yalu and his base at Antung.

'I quickly pulled in behind him, put my pipper on his tail pipe and almost had a kill. At that very instant I observed what appeared to be flaming ping-pong balls floating by my aircraft. I realised that they were cannon rounds from a MiG! I then heard, "'Cobra 4' break right now!" I had no choice but to break off.

'Later, we determined that the original two MiGs that had initially abandoned the fray had decided to come back and help. It was apparent that they had received a bit of

"encouragement" from the one that was being fired on! My hard break to the right probably saved my life, and luckily the MiGs did not follow us as we headed back to Suwon. At least Lt Col Ruddell got another kill, and his run of success would eventually net him eight MiGs.'

ACES HIGH!

When the ceasefire was signed on 27 July 1953, there were officially 39 pilots who had 'made ace' whilst flying the Sabre. In 2000 a 40th name was added to the list when Lt Gen Charles Cleveland joined the ranks of the aces. He had claimed four confirmed kills and a probable whilst serving as a 1st Lieutenant with the 4th FW's 334th FS in 1952. The Fighter Aces Board, after reviewing the gun camera film some 47 years after the war had ended, upgraded his probable to a confirmed victory.

Within this elite group of 40 pilots were 11 double aces. 1Lt Harold E Fischer was one of the latter, and had he not fallen victim to a split-second of bad luck, he might easily have been the top scorer of the war. Promoted to captain on 25 February 1953, he claimed his final victory on 21 March and was forced down behind enemy lines 17 days later. Fischer's policy was to shoot down every MiG he encountered, as that would be one less for him to fight the next time round! This code was ingrained in the minds of the more aggressive pilots that were flying F-86s in-theatre.

Here, Hal Fischer relates one of the many kills he claimed whilst on his way to becoming a double ace. He had already been in many dogfights by the time he downed this particular MiG, and the knowledge he had gained about how to fight the communist jet had earned him great respect from his fellow pilots;

'With the experience I had received over North Korea, it was inevitable that I would have the opportunity to score again. One afternoon, while waiting down at base operations, a call came in for a flight leader to race over to the group briefing room for a "hurry up" mission to search for a downed pilot that had reportedly crashed near the Yalu River. Four of us received the sketchiest of briefings, and since time was of the essence, we quickly took off and headed northwest.

'There was a lot of activity reported both north and south of the river, (*text continues on page 64*)

Two 39th FS F-86F-1s depart Suwon in a section take-off, bound for 'MiG Alley', in early 1953. The lead Sabre (51-2852) was the aircraft that Capt Harold Fischer was forced to bail out of on 7 April 1953 shortly after destroying two MiGs that he was never given official credit for. The 51st FW's ranking ace at the time of his demise, Fischer spent the next 25 months as a PoW (*Earl Shutt*)

1Lt Harold Fischer (centre) receives a lot of attention as he leaves the flightline after scoring his seventh and eighth MiG kills on 16 February 1953. He is wearing a yellow 39th FS cap and holding a blue 16th FS helmet (*Dean Abbott*)

COLOUR PLATES

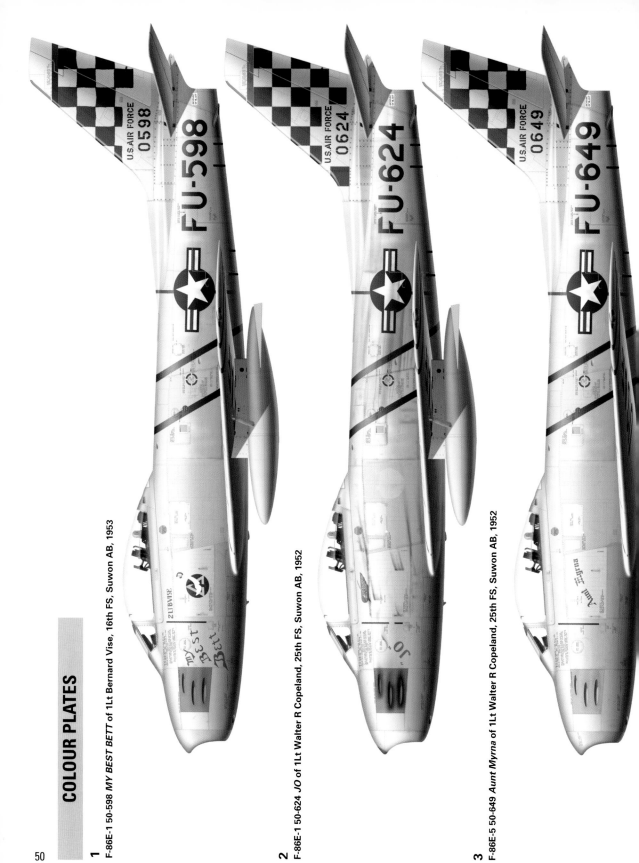

1
F-86E-1 50-598 *MY BEST BETT* of 1Lt Bernard Vise, 16th FS, Suwon AB, 1953

2
F-86E-1 50-624 *JO* of 1Lt Walter R Copeland, 25th FS, Suwon AB, 1952

3
F-86E-5 50-649 *Aunt Myrna* of 1Lt Walter R Copeland, 25th FS, Suwon AB, 1952

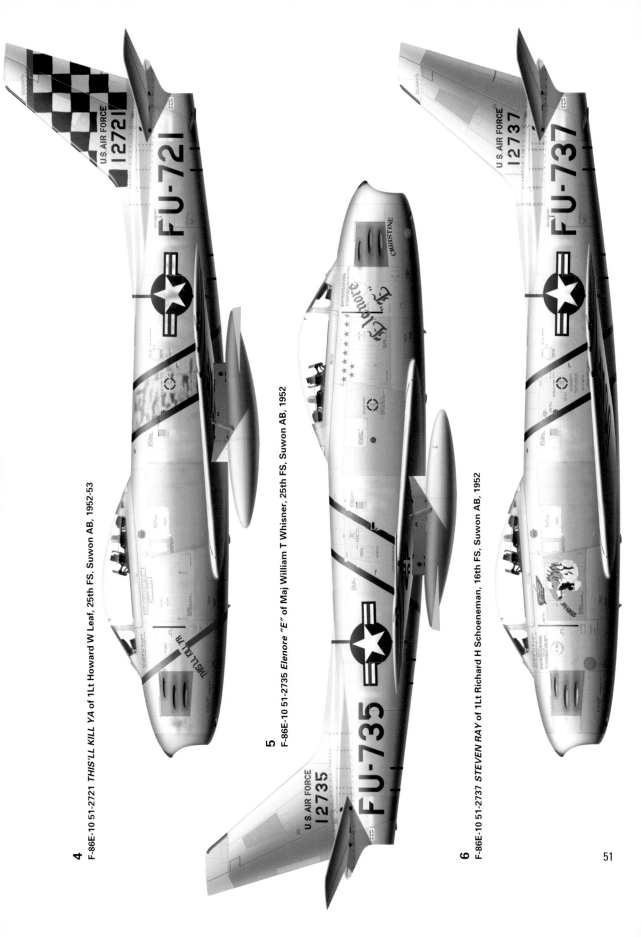

4
F-86E-10 51-2721 *THIS'LL KILL YA* of 1Lt Howard W Leaf, 25th FS, Suwon AB, 1952-53

5
F-86E-10 51-2735 *Elenore "E"* of Maj William T Whisner, 25th FS, Suwon AB, 1952

6
F-86E-10 51-2737 *STEVEN RAY* of 1Lt Richard H Schoeneman, 16th FS, Suwon AB, 1952

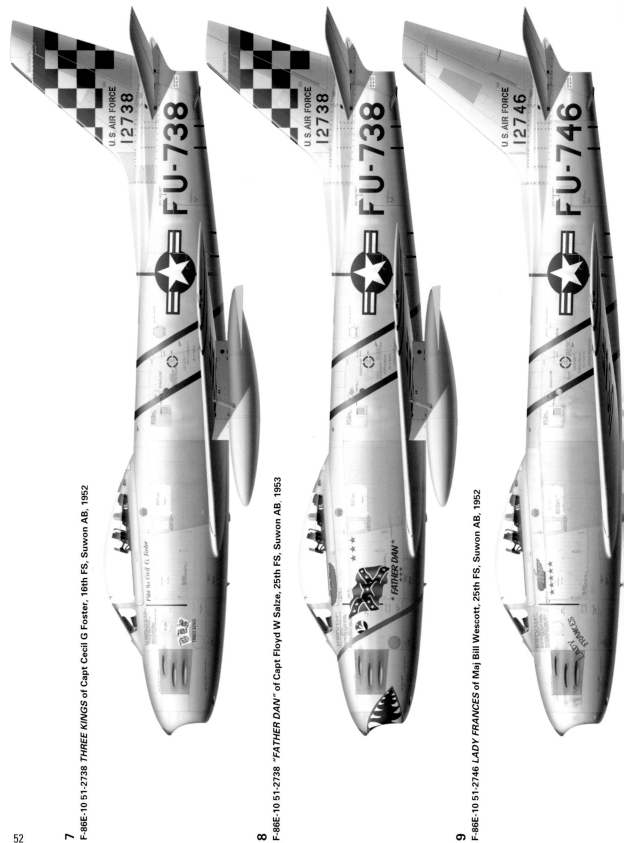

7
F-86E-10 51-2738 *THREE KINGS* of Capt Cecil G Foster, 16th FS, Suwon AB, 1952

8
F-86E-10 51-2738 *"FATHER DAN"* of Capt Floyd W Salze, 25th FS, Suwon AB, 1953

9
F-86E-10 51-2746 *LADY FRANCES* of Maj Bill Wescott, 25th FS, Suwon AB, 1952

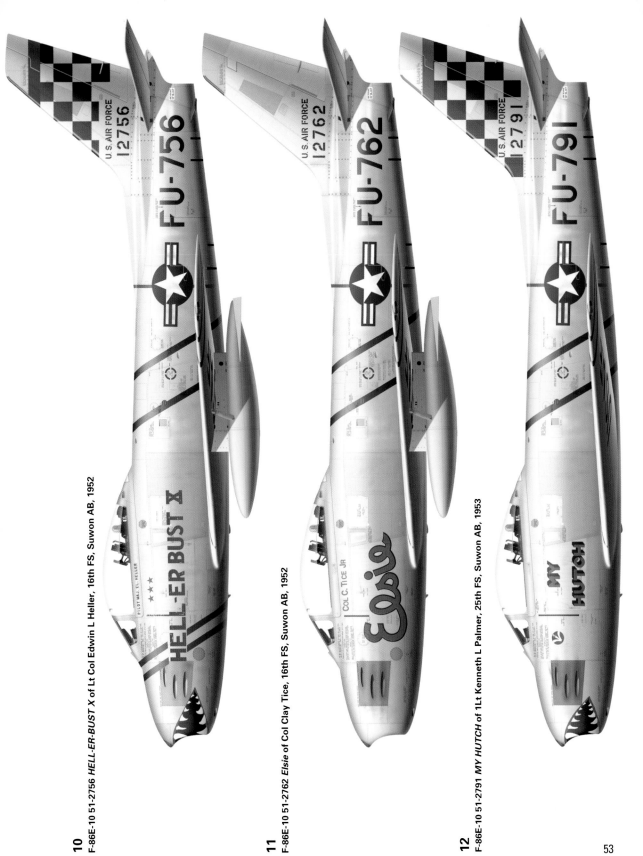

10

F-86E-10 51-2756 *HELL-ER-BUST X* of Lt Col Edwin L Heller, 16th FS, Suwon AB, 1952

11

F-86E-10 51-2762 *Elsie* of Col Clay Tice, 16th FS, Suwon AB, 1952

12

F-86E-10 51-2791 *MY HUTCH* of 1Lt Kenneth L Palmer, 25th FS, Suwon AB, 1953

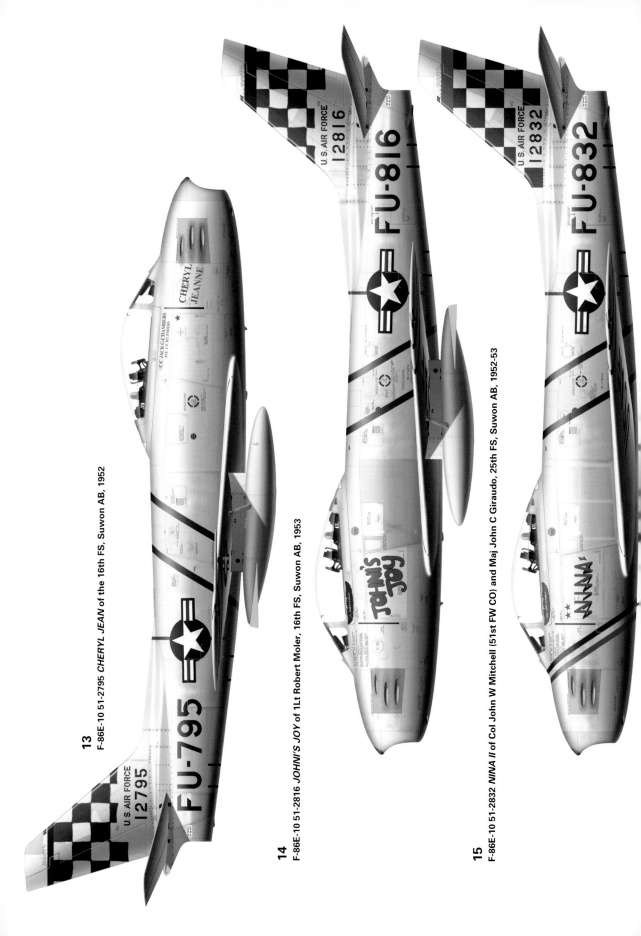

13

F-86E-10 51-2795 *CHERYL JEAN* of the 16th FS, Suwon AB, 1952

14

F-86E-10 51-2816 *JOHN'S JOY* of 1Lt Robert Moler, 16th FS, Suwon AB, 1953

15

F-86E-10 51-2832 *NINA II* of Col John W Mitchell (51st FW CO) and Maj John C Giraudo, 25th FS, Suwon AB, 1952-53

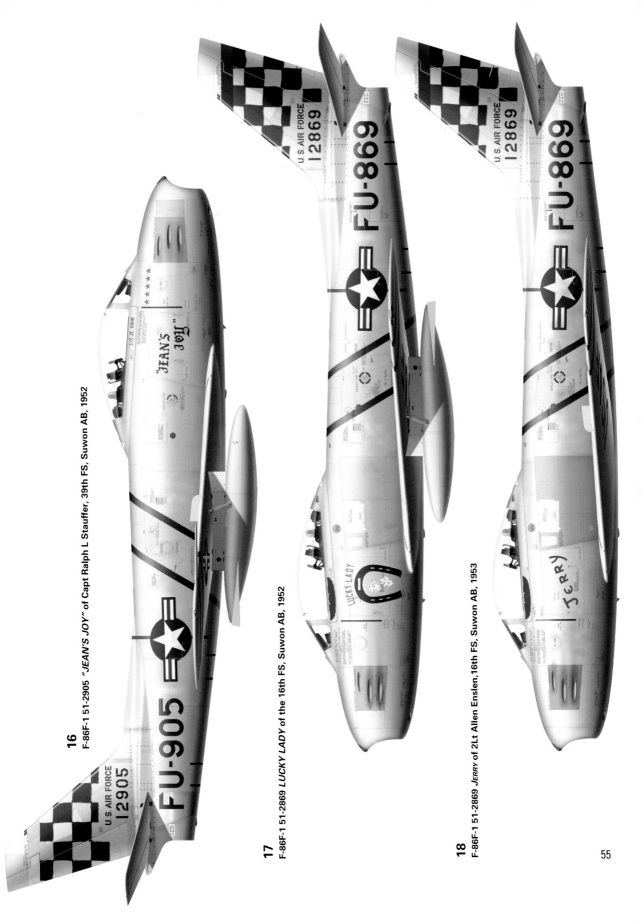

16
F-86F-1 51-2905 *"JEAN'S JOY"* of Capt Ralph L Stauffer, 39th FS, Suwon AB, 1952

17
F-86F-1 51-2869 *LUCKY LADY* of the 16th FS, Suwon AB, 1952

18
F-86F-1 51-2869 *JERRY* of 2Lt Allen Enslen, 16th FS, Suwon AB, 1953

55

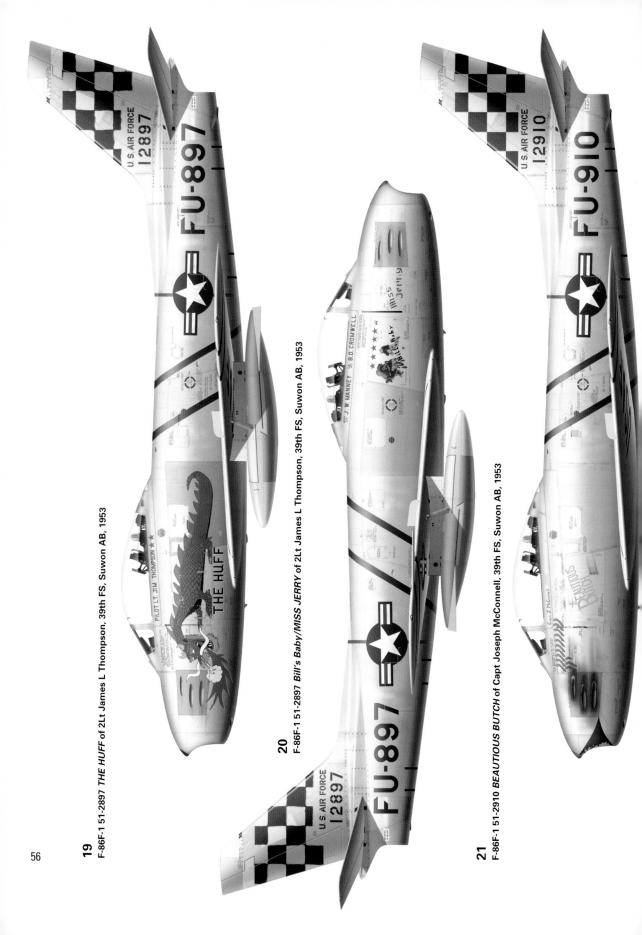

19
F-86F-1 51-2897 *THE HUFF* of 2Lt James L Thompson, 39th FS, Suwon AB, 1953

20
F-86F-1 51-2897 *Bill's Baby/MISS JERRY* of 2Lt James L Thompson, 39th FS, Suwon AB, 1953

21
F-86F-1 51-2910 *BEAUTIOUS BUTCH* of Capt Joseph McConnell, 39th FS, Suwon AB, 1953

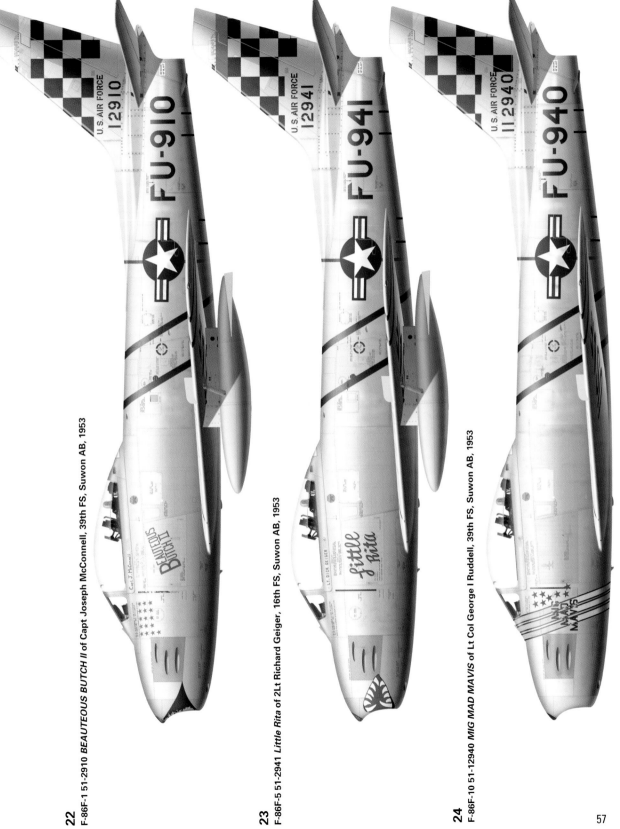

22
F-86F-1 51-2910 *BEAUTEOUS BUTCH II* of Capt Joseph McConnell, 39th FS, Suwon AB, 1953

23
F-86F-5 51-2941 *Little Rita* of 2Lt Richard Geiger, 16th FS, Suwon AB, 1953

24
F-86F-10 51-12940 *MIG MAD MAVIS* of Lt Col George I Ruddell, 39th FS, Suwon AB, 1953

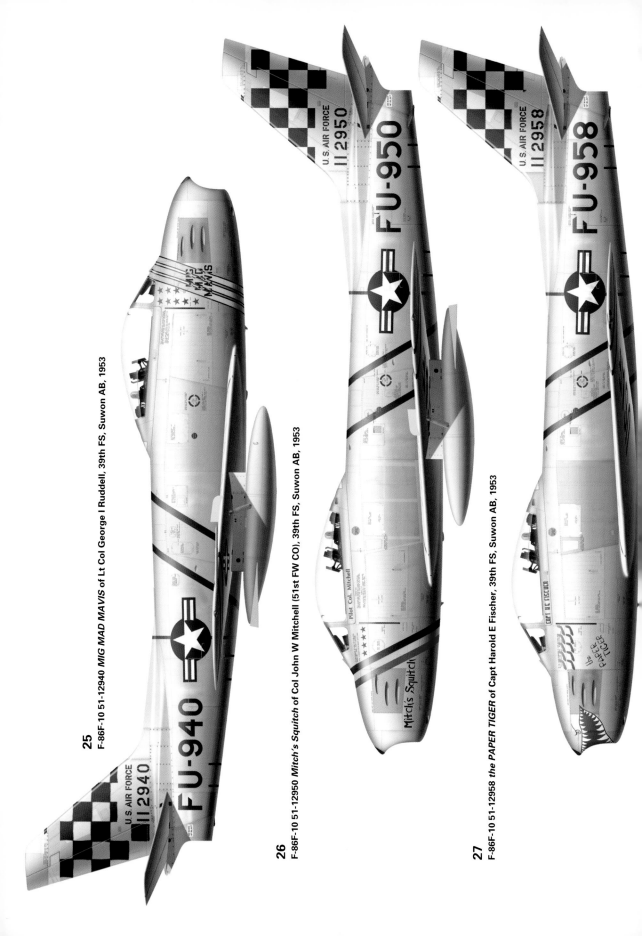

25
F-86F-10 51-12940 *MIG MAD MAVIS* of Lt Col George I Ruddell, 39th FS, Suwon AB, 1953

26
F-86F-10 51-12950 *Mitch's Squitch* of Col John W Mitchell (51st FW CO), 39th FS, Suwon AB, 1953

27
F-86F-10 51-12958 *the PAPER TIGER* of Capt Harold E Fischer, 39th FS, Suwon AB, 1953

28
F-86E-6(CAN) 52-2852 *DARLING DOTTIE* of Maj John F Bolt, 39th FS, Suwon AB, 1953

29
F-86E-6(CAN) 52-2867 *CHODO-MATTE* of 2Lt Hans Degner, 16th FS, Suwon AB, 1952-53

30
F-86E-6(CAN) 52-2889 *Jeanie* of Capt Howard Leaf, 25th FS, Suwon AB, 1953

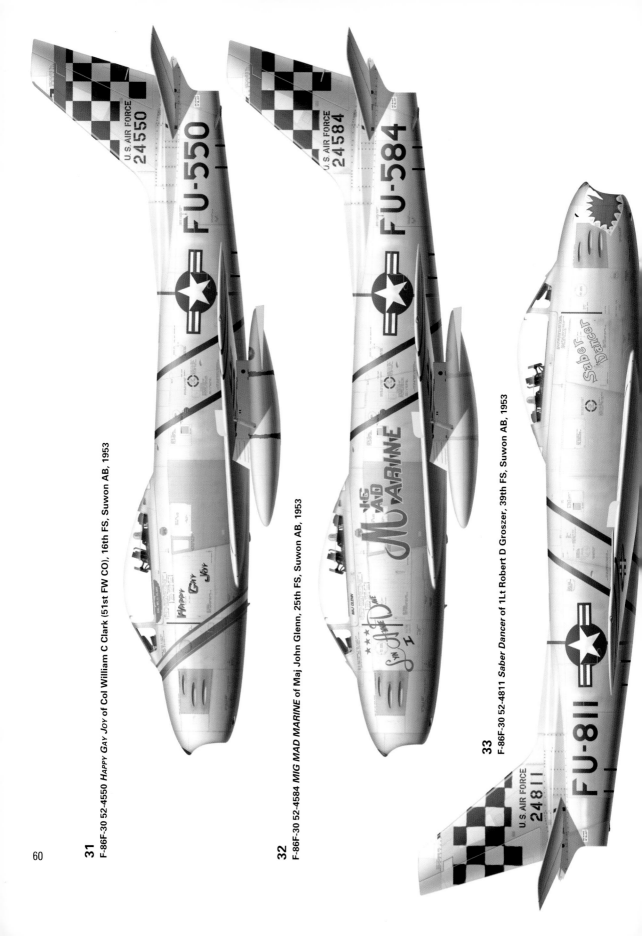

31

F-86F-30 52-4550 *HAPPY GAY JOY* of Col William C Clark (51st FW CO), 16th FS, Suwon AB, 1953

32

F-86F-30 52-4584 *MIG MAD MARINE* of Maj John Glenn, 25th FS, Suwon AB, 1953

33

F-86F-30 52-4811 *Saber Dancer* of 1Lt Robert D Groszer, 39th FS, Suwon AB, 1953

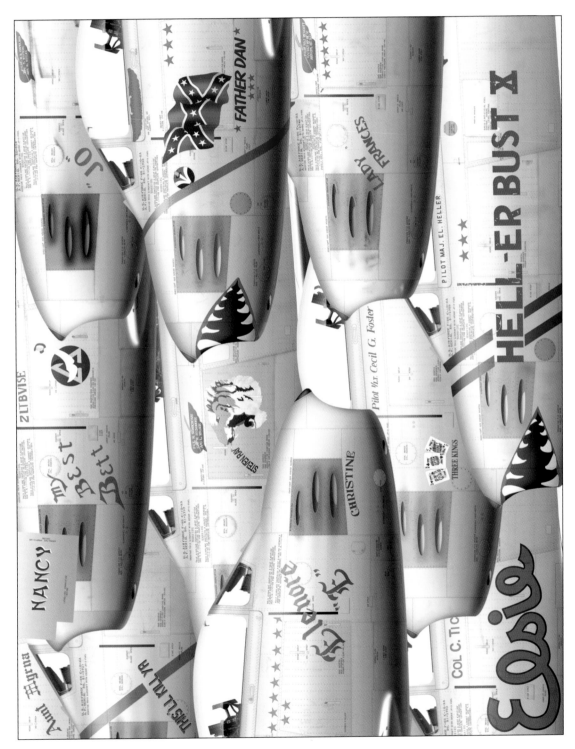

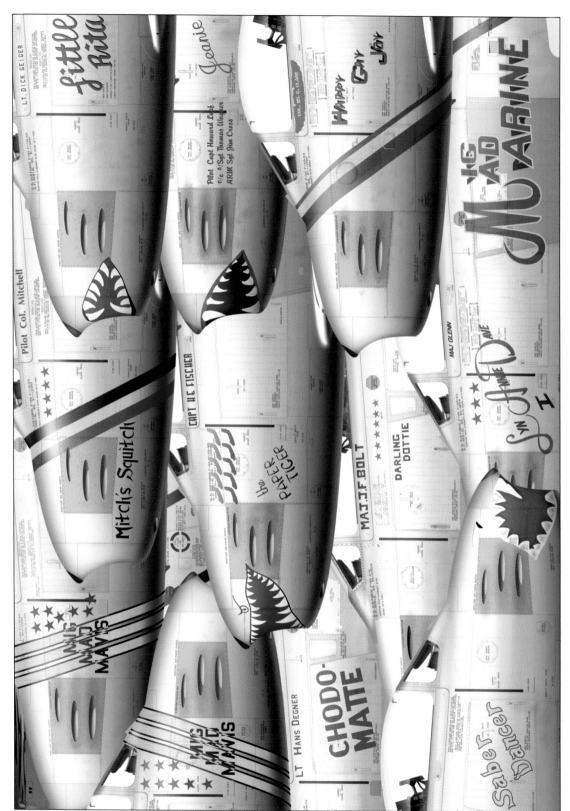

63

1Lt Harold Fischer (left) poses for a photograph with his crew chief on the 39th FS flightline in late 1952. The double ace flew one of the few sharkmouthed Sabres to be found in-theatre (*Harold Fischer*)

and again a feeling of intense excitement pulsed through me! Being subject to migraine headaches at times like these, the first indication I would get that one of these was imminent was distorted vision in my right eye. I always dreaded the possibility of suffering a migraine in flight, but fortunately this never happened while I was flying in Korea.

'As soon as we passed over the Chongchon River, we saw contrails approaching us from the south that were well above our altitude of 40,000 ft. Evidently, the enemy GCI stations were reporting effectively. The likelihood of impending action prior to us reaching the area to search for the downed pilot was high, so I called for our external tanks to be dropped. Seven of the eight tanks fell away, glittering in the sun as they headed earthward. It was standard operating procedure for an aircraft with a hung tank to be sent back to base with his escort. I ordered my wingman to escort the No 4 man back to Suwon. This left the element leader, Archie Tucker, and me alone to face the MiGs. Both of us had a lot of experience, so we were ready.

'About 20 miles north of the Chongchon, we found ourselves in a gold-fish bowl with MiGs all around us! Fortunately, when they appeared, none of them were in a good firing position, so we immediately started a turn to keep our tails clear. The MiG pilots had a tendency to fire at our aircraft if their noses were pointed vaguely in our direction. Since there was only a slim chance of them hitting us, it was no more than a little disconcerting. Both of us decided to at least squeeze off a few shots to upset them, and discourage their attack. Consequently, when the opportunity presented itself, we fired tracers in their general direction.

'Several chances came in rapid succession for attacks on the MiGs, but as soon as I started firing, Archie would call a break to fend off other MiGs that were attacking us. In a matter of minutes, we attacked and defended many times, with neither side gaining the advantage. It was only a matter of time before both sides had to withdraw. Evidently, the MiGs had less fuel than we did, so their superiority waned as they gradually withdrew. This gave us more of an opportunity to pursue our determined attack. Turning to the left, we dropped down on a flight of two jets that were heading for sanctuary north of the Yalu. We were up at 40,000 ft, and for the attack I positioned myself directly behind the MiG at the ideal range of 600 ft.

The USAF's 25th jet ace, Hal Fischer adorned his F-86F-10 (51-12958) with small MiG-15 silhouettes to mark his success in combat, rather than the more traditional red stars. This photograph was taken just prior to Fischer's loss over China on his 70th combat mission in F-86s (*Earl Shutt*)

'Before I could settle down to fire, the MiG pulled up and over in an almost perfect loop. My F-86 floundered around at the top of the loop, and I only made it because of the excessive speed I had brought with me coming into the attack. I fired off a burst just as Archie called out that he was down to "bingo" fuel. Having no intention of abandoning the chase, I told him to leave when he had to, but to let me know before he left!

'The MiG executed consecutive loops, and in so doing he passed the advantage to me as he lost altitude. Just over the Yalu, the MiG straightened out momentarily, and I was just preparing to fire a long burst when an object shot past my aircraft – it was the MiG's canopy, followed immediately by the pilot in his ejection seat! He had punched out, having evidently given up trying to shake off a determined F-86 that had no doubt been reported to him as being unable to follow a MiG in a loop at altitude! During the time I had been firing, I had not observed a hit register through my gunsight, and the only reason that I had fired was to disconcert him as much as possible. Fortunately, my gun camera film captured the pilot ejecting, and I was credited with the kill.'

FINAL ACES

Several of the Sabre pilots that only reached Korea in the last months of the war were able to achieve ace status because the hunting was very lucrative, especially during the May-June period. One such individual was 1Lt Henry Buttelmann of the 25th FS, who had arrived in-theatre in December 1952. For the first six months of his time in the frontline he flew as a wingman, but when he finally graduated to the shooter's slot, he made short work of becoming the USAF's 36th jet ace. Buttelmann recorded his first kill on 19 June and his fifth victory just 11 days later. He added two more to his tally in July to finish the war with seven kills.

Here, 'Hank' Buttelmann explains the processes that all new Sabre pilots went through in Korea, and what this training did for him;

'Upon my arrival in Korea I was sent to the 25th FS at Suwon AB. We had to complete at least five or six check rides in the Sabre before we could fly combat missions. My first mission up north came on 15 January 1953, and from that point on, I was a wingman for some of the more experienced pilots in the squadron. Once you had around 55 missions under your belt in this position, you would be made an element leader, which put you in a shooting position.

Kitted out in his survival gear, 1Lt Hank Buttelmann climbs into the cockpit of his 25th FS jet prior to flying yet another mission. The USAF's 36th jet ace, he was credited with seven kills (*USAF*)

'We were given some basic information about the MiG-15, but not too much was known about it at the time. We were told that it was much lighter than the Sabre, and that it could easily exceed the altitudes we could reach. We also knew that its heavy guns (23 mm and 37 mm cannon) had more killing power than our 0.50-cal weapons.

'My first MiG kill came on my very first flight (19 June 1953) as an element lead – I believe it was my 57th mission. That particular sortie was a routine sweep along the Yalu. We were on a normal patrol when I noticed a flight of MiGs well below us. At this time, most of the enemy fighters were flying at lower altitudes due to poor weather. We always patrolled at around 40,000 ft simply because we were some 220 miles from our base at Suwon with drop tanks on our jets.

'After we punched our tanks off, the MiGs appeared to change course and head for their base north of the river. I was behind my flight leader as he went in on the bounce. He had his speed brakes shut, so we came in very fast, but he misjudged the distance between us and rolled out way behind his target. When it became obvious to me that he was not closing on the MiGs, I popped my speed brakes open and slid in behind the closest enemy fighter. I gave the latter several short bursts and its canopy blew off. The pilot was still flying as if the canopy was still in place, however, so I gave him two more short bursts. The pilot then ejected, giving me a very quick, and easily confirmed, kill.'

The author has quizzed many of the F-86 pilots that saw action in the last six months of the war about the quality of the MiG pilots that they encountered. Buttelmann's reply was as follows;

'It would be hard for me to accurately evaluate the skill of these pilots simply because all of my encounters as a shooter came during the final few weeks of the war. I could only compare these individuals with the ones that were flying in early 1953. I do remember one encounter that I was more than happy with when it was all over, however!

'I was bounced by a MiG, but I was able to get him to overshoot me, and I immediately wound up in a scissors manoeuvre with him. This was not ideal when it came to fighting an agile MiG-15, but on this occasion I had no choice. After four or five scissors, I was able to stay with him, but we were losing altitude and airspeed. This pilot gave absolutely no sign of exiting the fight, and while I still had enough altitude and airspeed to dive away, I pulled

Wearing a flying helmet adorned with the 51st FW's legendary checkers, 1Lt Henry Buttelmann poses for the camera in this official photograph, taken soon after the ceasefire (*USAF*)

25th FS F-86F-30 52-4584 *MIG MAD MARINE* was assigned to Marine Corps exchange pilot Maj John Glenn. One of several Marine Corps aviators to fly with the 51st FW in Korea, Glenn claimed two kills in the last month of the conflict. He would later become a Mercury astronaut and then a US Senator (*USMC*)

out of the engagement because I felt he would have been able to out turn me. My other tangles with MiGs were much easier.'

When asked about the MiG-15's capabilities versus those of the F-86, all Sabre pilots stated that they felt they were flying the better fighter. At the cutting edge of technology in the early 1950s, they were then considered to be the best fighters in the world. Buttelmann stated;

'Of all the fighters I flew in the Air Force, including those during the

A 39th FS Sabre is readied for its next mission out on the Suwon flightline. The jet is being filled with JP-4 from the refuelling truck parked to the left of the photograph. The high-walled sandbag revetments are clearly visible in this shot (*Ron Wilson*)

Vietnam era, I can honestly say that the F-86 was probably the easiest, most forgiving and most fun aircraft I ever flew. The MiG-15 had certain advantages over the Sabre, but the communist pilots rarely exploited these in most cases because their training was vastly inferior to ours.'

Post-war, the reason why most MiG pilots failed to match their USAF counterparts in combat reached the west. Soviet/Warsaw Pact units sent to fight in Korea were swapped out on a regular basis, entire regiments being pulled from Manchuria and replaced by new ones. Therefore, the experience level built up by MiG pilots in-theatre during months of combat was lost when their unit returned home. Brand new regiments were forced to start from scratch, their pilots having to learn about tactics and the F-86's potential the hard way. Many lost their lives in the process.

One of the units to reap the benefit of this misguided policy was the 39th FS, and in particular its 'D' Flight. The latter always seemed to be in the thick of the action, and this was probably due to the fact that 'Mac' McConnell was its leader. Not all of the combat missions flown by Sabre squadrons saw them performing sweeps or combat air patrols. One of the lesser publicised missions was the early morning weather reconnaissance flight, which was regularly performed by 'D' Flight. 2Lt Gil Lowder was in 'Mac's' flight, and he recalled one of these early morning sorties;

'I was flying in the No 4 slot, and my element leader was Royal Canadian Air Force exchange pilot Flg Off Andy Lambrose. We began our mission on the east shore of the Yellow Sea, off the west coast of North Korea. The sky was bright blue and cloudless. As we approached the mouth of the Yalu, our radar facility called out three "trains" crossing the river, and they suggested that we leave the area. It appeared that other Sabres would be vectored in to intercept the MiGs. "Mac" made no radio transmission to drop our tanks. He just peeled them and we did the same.

'Looking to the east, we could see the "trains" of about ten aircraft each. They were in two-ship flights, one behind the other. There was a low group, and a second group that was about 2000 ft above and behind the first one. The last group had about the same separation. We were flying at about 45,000 ft in our F-86Fs. "Mac" began a shallow turn to the right, which I thought would intercept the high "train" at about their "five o'clock" position. He felt that an attack on the lower group would be the best way for us to inflict some damage, so we went after it. The MiGs split and "Mac" went after one and I stayed with my element lead as he took

Like the Marine Corps and the Royal Air Force, the Royal Canadian Air Force (RCAF) also sent a handful of pilots over to Korea to fly combat missions with the two Sabre fighter wings in-theatre. One of those individuals was Flt Lt William W Fox of the 16th FS, who is seen here taking it easy between missions. The most successful RCAF pilot to serve with the USAF in terms of the number of MiGs he downed was Flt Lt Ernest A Glover of the 4th FW's 334th FS, who claimed three destroyed in 1952. The 51st FW's leading Canadian pilot was Sqn Ldr James D Lindsay, who bagged two jets whilst flying with the 39th FS (*James Lindsay*)

off after another one. Several MiGs made firing passes on us, and I was able to call out the breaks at the right time. Their tactics and firing passes indicated they were probably in the final phase of their training cycle.

'While Flg Off Lambrose and I were trying to cover each other in this free-for-all, we suddenly had a call from "Mac's" wingman, 1Lt George Benedict. He had been jumped by some MiGs and had his hands full. He indicated that he was down on the deck, and a MiG-15 instructor pilot was on his rear, refusing to be shaken off. We both split off from our MiGs and headed down to help Benedict. Before we could get to him, he radioed that he had lost his MiG, so we all joined up and headed south. This was a typical mission for us in that the MiGs fired lots of rounds and didn't hit us, and we didn't have much of a chance to manoeuvre around and get shots at them. There were no kills on either side.'

While a significant number of missions were flown where no shots were fired, the sheer size of the F-86 formation often had a lot to do with whether the MiGs would come down off their 'perch' and fight. Should a flight be forced to lose jets due to technical failures, the remaining two-ship element could provide a tempting target for the enemy. And with all Sabre units in-theatre strictly adhering to the rule that when an aircraft had a problem on a mission, its pilot would immediately return to base along with his wingman, enemy radar soon detected the emasculated Sabre formations. 2Lt Lowder flew one such mission with 'Mac' McConnell, and they soon found themselves in a precarious situation;

'Capt McConnell was our flight leader on a sweep along the Yalu. I was flying on his wing, and we were with another element which suffered a technical failure that forced them to turn south while we were still some distance away from the patrol area. We were climbing through 45,000 ft when I noticed what I thought was a "spare" aircraft joining our element. It didn't alarm me because our radar site had not called out any MiGs in the area, and we still were not in their "zone".

'We had not flown far enough to test fire our guns when I noticed the "spare" was test firing his. Somehow, the pattern of smoke coming from the gun ports was different from that normally associated with an F-86, and that was when it hit me that the "spare" was in fact a MiG-15! I immediately called out to "Mac" to break right, and told him that he had a bandit firing from his "six o'clock" position. He radioed me back to tell me that the MiG wasn't firing at him, but at me! I looked back behind me, and sure enough there was a second MiG at close range, firing away at me. His tracer rounds looked like flaming baseballs coming toward me.

'I yanked back on the stick and said a quick prayer that he would miss. As we were locked up in a maximum-G turn, "Mac" told me to ease up, but with that MiG blazing away I wasn't about to ease up! Tighter and tighter I pulled, and after a few seconds I glanced back and the MiG was gone, and so was "Mac". He had come around and blown it off my tail without me realising. This was his 12th kill.

'When we got back to Suwon, I asked him why he wanted me to ease up. He replied that the bandit was so close, and we were pulling so many Gs, that his gunsight pipper was on my tailpipe as he was pouring lead into the MiG! I never found out what happened to the first MiG that had fired at me. This was an unusual mission in that we were jumped long before we reached the area where we thought the enemy would be.'

OTHER MEMORABLE MISSIONS

Many missions flown in Korea by wingmen and other pilots that did not achieve ace status were often just as exciting, and occasionally more dangerous, than those flown by the high-scorers. While the aces accounted for approximately 95 of the 303 kills made by the 51st FW, a large number of relatively unknown pilots fought it out with some of the best MiG instructors based north of the Yalu River. A significant number of the new pilots assigned to the wing in 1952-53 blossomed into some of the best dogfighters within months of their arrival in-theatre. Fresh out of flying training, they learned their trade whilst serving as wingmen for the more experienced flight leads.

Not all new pilots survived, however, with a small number falling victim to the heavy-calibre cannons of the MiG-15. Others suffered mechanical failures in their war-weary Sabres deep into enemy territory. Some pilots were rescued, but a number became PoWs or were killed outright. Amongst of the latter was 25th FS pilot Capt Floyd W Salze.

An exceptional Sabre pilot who had previously seen combat in World War 2, he had joined the 51st FW with two Me 262 kills to his credit from his time flying P-51Ds in the ETO in 1944-45. Quickly made a flight lead, Salze had destroyed two MiG-15s by early June 1953. Looking for his fifth kill during a mission over 'MiG Alley' on 11 June, his luck ran out when his jet suffered an engine failure. His wingman, 1Lt Robert R Brackett, recalls details of this fateful flight;

'We had been briefed to fly top cover for an RF-80 photo-reconnaissance mission. We were to fly along the Yalu River from west to east. Capt Salze was our flight leader, and as he led us out to the main

25TH FS F-86F-10 51-2738 *FATHER DAN* cruises at altitude toward the MiG hunting grounds in northwest Korea. The aircraft was named after the 51st FW Chaplain, Father Dan Campbell. It survived the war and went on to serve with the 35th FW in Japan (*Sam Young*)

runway, we saw our wing chaplain, Father Dan Campbell. He was always out there to salute us, and give each of us the sign of the cross as we went to full throttle. Father Dan was a well liked fixture within the wing, and Capt Salze even named his Sabre after him.

'We launched without any problems and had soon made visual contact with the recce jet. As the RF-80 made its photo run, there was some scattered flak but nothing noteworthy, for it was far below us. I don't think the flak had anything to do with Salze's engine failure. Soon after heading back to Suwon, his jet lost power. All four of our Sabres were already below "Bingo" fuel, so our Nos 3 and 4 headed back, while Capt Salze told me that he was going to aim for the open water of the Yellow Sea, where he would have a chance of being rescued. His efforts to re-start his engine failed as we headed into lower cloud layers. I slipped in behind him to help him keep gliding in the right direction on instruments.

F-86E-10 51-2791 *MY HUTCH* was assigned to 1Lt Kenneth Palmer of the 25th FS during the final months of the war. He was credited with a solitary MiG-15 kill in this jet on 29 June 1953 (*Ken Palmer*)

F-86F-10 51-2793 *Jackie's Jag* was being flown by the 25th FS when this photograph was taken, but during its lengthy combat tour it was assigned, at one time or another, to each of the three squadrons within the 51st FW. The jet also served with the 35th FW post-war

'We broke out over open water at about 10,000 ft, and Salze punched out. I made a wide circle around him, and he waved to me that everything was okay. I then proceeded back to Suwon, knowing that a rescue helicopter had him spotted. What happened next was a tragedy for both Capt Salze and the helicopter pilot. The underpowered machine tried to lift Salze up three times and failed because he was still attached to his 'chute. Finally the helicopter had to back off and allow an SA-16 Dumbo floatplane to

come in and pick him up, but by that time Salze had already drowned.'

Salze had bagged his second MiG-15 less than a week before this mission. With time still left in his tour, he might have gone on to become an ace, but that chance never came.

WINGMEN

Some of the best shooters in-theatre were the less experienced wingmen, but due to a rigid code in the air, they passed up the opportunity to engage MiGs in order to protect their leader. Occasionally, flight leads exhausted their ammunition, however, allowing the wingman to secure the kill.

While flying as wingmen had to be frustrating for these younger pilots, they learned from the best, and that ensured another generation of disciplined, well-trained fighter pilots that could hold their own against any adversary. 1Lt Philip C Davis finished his combat tour with MiG kills and 112 missions to his credit. He worked his way up to a shooter's position, which meant that he had logged many hours over 'MiG Alley' as a wingman. He learned his trade from some of the best Sabre pilots in the 51st FW, including group CO, and ace, Col Robert P Baldwin, and future 16th FS CO, Maj Ed Heller;

'As a young lieutenant, and wingman, I was privileged to be able to fly with Maj Ed Heller. He was the ultimate fighter pilot, and a great teacher. On one particularly memorable mission (on 17 November 1952), one of the pilots in our flight had a hung wing tank, and the rules dictated that he and his wingman

The 51st's Operations building at Suwon AB (*Wayne Rose*)

World War 2 Mustang ace Lt Col Edwin Heller (left) was commanding officer of the 16th FS when he was shot down and captured on 25 January 1953. He had claimed 3.5 MiGs destroyed by the time of his demise. Here, he shakes hands with his crew chief, Sgt Clio Morales. Like his fighters in World War 2, Heller's Sabre was named *HELL-ER BUST* (*USAF*)

had to leave the patrol and return to base. This left Maj Heller and I as a two-ship. We were at 35,000 ft and headed in the direction of Antung at the time, although we were still south of the Yalu River .

'As we passed the "Mizou" (Suiho Reservoir), we spotted two MiG-15s in close formation just ahead and below us. Heller called the bounce and I assumed the protective position below and aft of him. The major opened fire at 800 ft and both MiGs pulled up and to the left, with Heller still firing. He was getting good hits on MiG No 1, which broke left and down, while MiG No 2 continued up and to the left, which was perfect for me to get a shot in. However, as a good wingman, my job was to stay with my lead, and for a split-second I wrestled with this dilemma, before deciding I had better stick to the rules. This proved to be a dumb move.

'MiG No 2 immediately dropped in behind me and started shooting balls of fire in my direction. I pulled up as hard as an F-86 could take without losing it. Hunkering down behind the armour plate behind the seat, I kept repeating to myself, "He can't hit me, he can't hit me", and he didn't. After approximately 720 degrees of high-G turning, I eased up and MiG No 2 was nowhere to be seen. Miraculously, I found Maj Heller as soon as I rolled out, and once I had joined up with him, we headed back to Suwon. My leader had claimed his first MiG kill, and if I'd chosen to break the wingman's code, I might have got one too. However, my mission priorities were correct.

'My first kill came in April 1953. At this time I was "C" flight leader in the 16th FS. You had to have a tremendous amount of combat experience to lead, and I had already logged 80 missions. I had had several opportunities to score while flying wing, but due to the fact that I considered myself an excellent fighter pilot and a lousy shot, I had fumbled a few of the chances that presented themselves. I was now determined to get some kills even if I had to ram them!

'We always started out in flights of four, but on numerous occasions we would end up as an element of two. Usually, this was because someone in the flight had a "hung tank" and his wingman had to escort him out of the area so that he would not fall victim to a MiG attack. This would halve the flight's strength, and on the day in question, this is exactly what happened. My wingman (2Lt John W Goodwill) and I continued the patrol, and we turned down the Yalu at 40,000 ft.

'Shortly after we rolled out of our turn, I spotted a single MiG ahead and slightly below us, on a parallel course. I called the bounce and told my wingman to cover me. Letting down and closing, my range finder dropped from 1200 ft to 1000 ft and then to 800 ft. At this point I gave him a quick burst from my six 0.50-cal guns. I don't believe he had seen me until I started firing. There were numerous hits on the MiG, and I think he flamed out right after absorbing that first round. His fighter started emitting heavy white vapour from the tailpipe. We were definitely below the "cons", so I knew he was in trouble.

'Without wasting any time, he rolled over into a vertical dive, and I was right behind him, firing short bursts while we went straight down. When my altimeter rapidly approached the 10,000-ft mark, I began to get worried about being able to pull out. At that instant he initiated what must have been a 7- or 8-G pull out. I know this is accurate because I was pulling almost 7 Gs, and I watched him disappear out the top of my

The harsh winters in Korea are still vividly remembered by those that fought in the war. Huge storms swept south from Manchuria, literally blanketing the whole country with several feet of snow. This photograph of the 16th FS flightline was taken right after a major storm had hit Suwon in January 1953 (*Allen Enslen*)

windscreen (with my chin on my chest). While the G forces did not black me out, I could not hold my head up. We ended up in an almost vertical zoom, and then he abruptly rolled off and dove into the ground!

'In retrospect, I believe one of my early bursts may have killed or disabled the pilot, and the subsequent dive, pull out and final dive may have been the airframe's response to him slumping against the controls.

Midway through the encounter, my wingman began yelling that another MiG was trying to get on my tail. As we subsequently realised, this was a standard MiG tactic, where a second jet would be positioned about three miles in trail, ready to jump you while you were engaging his leader. I have always wondered how they talked their pilots into leading!'

1Lt Davis started looking for his wingman around the time that his MiG was making its fatal dive. Although he could not visually acquire him, he could hear him clearly on the radio. Davis finally shook the second MiG, and both Sabre pilots independently exited the area at high speed due to their low fuel states. In consideration for his harrowing experience, and a reward for keeping MiG No 2 off him, Davis split the kill with 2Lt Goodwill. This was teamwork taken to the highest level!

The MiG pilots were masters of a variety of tricks and deceptions, and although the Sabre pilots drastically out-scored their communist counterparts, these victories were often difficult to achieve thanks to the tactics being employed. It usually fell to the wingman to figure out exactly what the MiG pilots were up to, and then warn the element's shooter as the latter concentrated on his quarry. And Sabre pilots rarely enjoyed the element of surprise thanks to the MiG-15's better performance above 45,000 ft.

However, for 1Lt Davis's second victory, the communist fighter's superiority at high altitude was never a concern;

'My other kill was more routine than spectacular. It came during the early summer of 1953, when the war was rapidly winding down and we were primarily involved in routine patrols over the mouth of the Yalu River. On this mission, we were up at around 42,000 ft. We had just started an easy turn to the south – at that altitude, you had to be smooth and easy in order to keep your mach number up. Midway through the turn, I spotted a single MiG-15 heading south from its base at Antung. It was travelling at a high mach down at about 5000 ft. We did not hesitate as I called the bounce, opened the canopy defroster, chopped the power and headed downhill!

'I rapidly closed to his "six o'clock", holding off about 800 ft behind him. Unless this was a trap, we had the element of surprise, because the pilot had not taken any evasive action. We were always wary of any tricks or traps the MiG pilots might pull. He was perfectly lined up, and I squeezed off a quick burst which scored hits all over the fuselage. The MiG pilot instantly broke to the left and up, and I followed. We were both pulling four- or five-G, and I managed to pull harder and gradually got a good lead on him. Another quick burst from my guns ensured more strikes. I found myself yelling for him to go ahead and "blow up". At that instant, the pilot ejected. I was still firing, completely oblivious to his ejection, until my wingman, 2Lt Alvin Bouchard, called out for me to stop. I finally realised that the MiG was pilotless and broke off. We immediately headed back to Suwon, as there just wasn't much MiG activity in the air at that time.'

RULE BREAKERS

On paper, the rules and regulations about flying north of the Yalu River were pretty rigid, and many squadron commanders had no tolerance for violations. However, far more MiGs went down in their 'safe zone' than

Lt Gen Glenn O Barcus, commander of the Fifth Air Force, flew several combat missions with the 51st FW. He is seen here in F-86F-10 51-2951, which was on strength with the 39th FS at Suwon (*Clyde Wade*)

A close-up of the artwork that adorned F-86F-10 51-2951 *BARCUS CARCUSS*. The jet was always available for Lt Gen Barcus's use whenever he visited the 51st FW. Between visits, the Sabre was normally flown by pilots of the 39th FS (*Archie Shaw*)

will ever be known. Scores of communist jets limped back to base with heavy damage after the F-86 pilots broke off the pursuit at the river and were never able to make it back. Many MiG pilots were killed as they attempted to land their stricken fighters, while others punched out north of their bases out of sight of any gun camera film.

F-86 pilots routinely returned from missions with their gun camera film showing kills made over Manchuria, but they were denied credit for them as the penalty for flying over Chinese territory was far worse than being grounded. A good example of an aggressive Sabre pilot losing a kill because of the river boundary is explained here by 1Lt Ronald Wilson, who flew F-86Fs with the 39th FS;

'We experienced mixed emotions on the day that we encountered our MiGs. It was crystal clear, and there would be no weather problems to contend with, but conversely we were throwing heavy, persistent, contrails out behind us that made us feel like we were in clear view of anyone in the immediate area. This was my 32nd combat mission, and I was still flying the worst wing position of them all – No 4, or "tail-end Charlie". If the flight was attacked, it was usually the No 4 that got fired on first.

'We were flying the standard "fingertip" formation. The rules for these missions had not changed since the war started. If the flight

Possibly the most colourful Sabre to see combat in Korea was F-86F-1 51-2897 *THE HUFF*, flown by 1Lt James Thompson. He claimed two kills while flying this aircraft, one of which was a MiG-15 that had a dragon painted down the side. Thompson's crew chief then adorned the Sabre with artwork. *THE HUFF* was assigned to the 39th FS (*Archie Shaw*)

***THE HUFF* featured the titling *Bill's Baby* and this unusual artwork on its starboard side, as well as six kill symbols (*Harold Chitwood*)**

was separated, each element would stay together and fight. If the element broke up, we were required to terminate any combat and return to base.

'Since we were in the 39th FS, which was known as "The Flying Cobras", our call-signs featured snake names. On this particular day, we were "Cobra" flight. This mission took place in the early morning and our plan was to arrive at the Yalu at the highest altitude possible (45,000 ft), while trying to conserve as much fuel as we could. When we arrived, the sky was full of contrails, so there was going to be a lot of action. We could not tell who had made them, or how long they had been there.

'We were not the only Sabres up that day, and within minutes the radios were crackling with pilots calling in bandits and taking bounces on the enemy. You could hear the strain in their voices, especially when they were pulling Gs. Everyones' head was on a swivel. The next thing I heard was "Cobra Flight, Drop tanks!" We all punched off our externals, which were already empty, and a second later I heard "Cobra Flight, Break Left" and the fight was on.

'As I was No 4 on the left of the flight, the turn was in to me, which was difficult for me to perform. However, I managed to maintain contact with my element leader, but when we rolled out there were no other aircraft in sight. Having lost some altitude, we proceeded to climb back up as quickly as possible. About halfway through the climb, I spotted four MiGs above us and called out to my leader. He was up at about their level, and turned to take a bounce on the last one in the formation. As soon as he fired, the MiGs scattered in all directions. I stayed in my wing position to keep my leader clear from behind. I saw him scoring hits on the trailing aircraft that had turned north for a high-speed run for the safety of the river.

'Lead radioed me that he had fired out, and that I should take over the pursuit, which I did. We were less than 2000 ft behind, and were closing slightly, but the MiG was climbing, making it difficult for us to stay with him. I proceeded to fire and made numerous hits on him, causing the MiG to smoke and lose altitude. By this time, he was north of the river, and maybe we were too. I saw him continue to dive and smoke, and he eventually crashed into the ground, but my leader did not see it, so it was declared a "probable". By this time I had also fired out, and we were both low on fuel, so we headed home. Had this engagement started further to the south, the MiG would have gone down over North Korea and my leader would have seen it. I could have then claimed a kill.'

PLAYING CATCH-UP

The 16th and 25th FSs had got the jump on the 39th FS when it came to MiG kills as they had both received Sabres six months prior to the latter squadron. Indeed, when the 51st FW started its Korean tour with the F-86E, the 39th was still attached to the 18th FBW flying F-51D Mustangs in the close air support and interdiction roles. However, the scoring gap that existed between the three units was rapidly reduced when the 39th FS received the first F-models assigned to the 51st.

One of the newer pilots posted into the squadron soon after the arrival of the F-86Fs was 2Lt Al Duc. He recounted to the author some of the more memorable missions he flew in Korea with the likes of 'Mac' McConnell, John Bolt and Paul Jones;

Capt Joe McConnell (left) recalls a humourous incident during one of his missions for the press while fellow high-scoring ace Capt 'Pete' Fernandez of the 4th FW looks on with amusement. Having both just been removed from the frontline after exceeding their 100-mission quotas, the aces are seen here attending a press conference on 22 May 1953 after receiving DFCs for their outstanding accomplishments in the F-86 (*Bill Graski*)

F-86F-1 51-2869 *MY WONDERFUL GWEN* served with both the 16th and the 39th FSs during its time in Korea. Originally assigned to the 16th's 1Lt Allen Enslen, the jet carried the name *Jerry* on its port side (*Robert Mount*)

'The first MiG killer that I flew wing with was Capt Paul Jones. Before I sortied with him, he told me that when you are on a combat mission in MiG territory, keep a sharp eye out. "They can't hit you if you see them first".

'On about my third or fourth mission, wing CO Col John Mitchell was leading and I was flying wing for Capt Jones in the No 4 slot. MiGs were called out at "five o'clock high", and at the leader's command, the flight broke to the right into the MiGs and "BOOM"! Our lead had taken a hit in his left wing. The fight lasted for only a brief time, and we then flew back to base.

'This incident caused me to question what Jones had told me, because I took a look at Col Mitchell's Sabre when we got back and I could almost stand up through the hole left by the MiG's 37 mm cannon round. Although we had seen them right before they struck, we still could not avoid the hit. This gave me more incentive to keep my head on a swivel, as I endeavoured to see them far enough out in order to manoeuvre away from their gunsights.

'Capt Joe McConnell was my next flight commander. He had previously flown in another squadron, and had not yet made a name for himself. He was flight commander of "D" Flight within the 39th, and it was here that he made all 16 of his kills. Many people have asked me how he got all those victories, and I tell them that as well as being very aggressive, he had the perfect eyes for a fighter pilot. He could spot MiGs long before any one else in the flight.

'For example, the MiGs would often fly in what we referred to as a "train", which meant they were in trail, with about a mile or two separating each aircraft. There were usually eight aircraft in a "train". It

seemed that McConnell could always tell when the "train" had passed, and he would then position himself on the last MiG in the strung-out formation.

'Another tactic we used was called "trolling". Atmospheric conditions dictated if this tactic could be used. Flying the hard-wing F-86Fs allowed us to fly most of our missions at 45,000+ ft. If, by chance (and it happened often), aircraft started making contrails at about 40,000 ft and then ceased at about 45,000 ft, then "trolling" could be used. In this case, lead would get his second element to cruise at an

altitude of 42,000 ft (pulling "cons") while the lead element would climb above 45,000 ft, which put them out of the contrails and a short distance behind the second element flying below.

'The "troll" was now set up and in place, with the No 2 man keeping lead and himself cleared while lead kept the second element clear. If all went according to plan, the MiGs would spot the contrails and set up an attack. Lead was usually the first to pick up the bandits, and being at a higher altitude, he was able to close in and stay with the MiGs. It was also up to him to tell the second element when to turn or break, and in what direction, even if Nos 3 and 4 had the bandits in sight. When the element broke would usually determine if the attack will be successful or not. An early break would take the leader longer to close the gap, allowing the MiGs to call off their attack. A late break could overexpose Nos 3 and 4 to the danger of being shot down.'

The two types of missions flown mostly by Sabre fighter squadrons were CAP escort and fighter sweeps. The former meant that you were always on the defensive and the MiGs were the aggressors that could strike at any time from superior altitudes. Fighter sweeps were the pilots' favourite, as they were now on the offensive, looking to initiate a fight. 2Lt Duc reflected on these missions;

'The toughest mission type for me was always the CAP escort. By far, the best were the sweeps. Being a commander of an escort mission carried with it a lot of responsibility. First, you had to maintain a greater

Capt Joe McConnell signs his post-mission report forms after his eventful final sortie with the 39th FS on 18 May 1953. Flying F-86F-1 51-2910, he had claimed three MiG-15s destroyed and a fourth damaged during the course of the mission. Note the powder residue on the gun ports, signifying that he had fired his guns (Ron Wilson)

Although pilots that were manning the alert jets had to stay close by their F-86s, they could still have some fun if the weather was good – these 39th FS pilots are engaged in a game of 'Horseshoes' at Suwon. Note that the jet in the immediate background is already attached to a start cart just in case (Dean Abbott)

Ranking Korean War ace Capt Joe McConnell poses for the cameras with his crew chief and his final Sabre, F-86F-1 51-2910 *BEAUTEOUS BUTCH II*, several days after the photograph that appears atop page 78. Note that the 13 MiG silhouette victory markings have been replaced by freshly applied red stars below the jet's cockpit. Removed from the frontline on the direct orders of Lt Gen Barcus, Joe McConnell returned to the US and became involved in test flying with the Air Force. Having survived 106 combat missions, he was killed on 24 August 1954 at Edwards AFB, in California, while carrying out a routine acceptance test flight on brand new F-86H-1 52-1981. When the aircraft suffered hydraulic failure in flight, McConnell called on his vast experience from his time in Korea. Whilst in-theatre, he had routinely practised landing with just the throttle and rudder, and he tried this technique once again. It almost worked. However, ground turbulence lifted up a wing when he was seconds away from landing and the ace was forced to eject. McConnell, who was far too close to the ground, died on impact (*USAF*)

speed than the fighter-bombers you were protecting, or you would be at a big disadvantage if you were jumped by MiGs. Secondly, to maintain this higher speed, you had to weave, or zigzag. This meant turning most of the time, which made it hard to keep your objective in sight.

'The MiGs could use two aircraft and disrupt an entire flight of 48 fighters-bombers simply by flying through, or near, their gaggle. Even if they didn't fire a shot, but they caused the bomber pilots to jettison their bombs, they had accomplished their mission. Or, those same two could be trying to draw us away from the main strike force, allowing the main gaggle of MiGs to descend and shoot down several bombers. It was a big temptation to chase those MiGs that we saw below us!

'I can recall late one afternoon after a mission near the end of my combat tour, I noticed two RF-80s parked in our squadron's revetments. That evening at the Officer's Club, I spotted a pilot (1Lt Guy McSweeny) who was a fellow alumnus from flight school. He had flown one of the photo-ships down from Kimpo, and we were going to escort them into MiG territory. I was to lead one of the missions, and my classmate made sure he was on that sortie. One of the RF-80s would be flying a photo mission up on the Chongchon River, which meant a very short flight. The toughest one would be led by me, and it called for the photo bird to go all the way up to the Yalu River to take pictures of a B-29 bombing raid conducted the previous night. Intelligence needed to know how much damage had been done to the target.

'The mission was uneventful until the RF-80 came off his photo run. Going in, we paralleled the west coast until we came to the mouth of the Yalu. At this time, the photo-ship had started a slow descent to pick up speed. After he took the pictures and headed back east, I felt we had gotten through another one unscathed. At that time, McSweeny radioed us wanting to know where all the aircraft had come from. Picking him up after rolling out of a turn, there he was sitting in the middle of at least four

The 51st FW always boasted a handful of exchange pilots within its ranks, these aviators having come from the RAF, RCAF or the Marine Corps. Having often seen combat prior to arriving at Suwon, they soon became flight leads. The most successful of these 'imports' was Maj John Bolt, who is seen here enjoying a 'Bud' between sorties. Having claimed six 'Zekes' in the Pacific in 1943-44 whilst flying F4U-1/1A Corsairs as one of 'Pappy' Boyington's famous 'Black Sheep', Bolt had already completed a combat tour with the Marine Corps in Korea when he managed to wangle a posting to the 51st FW's 39th FS in 1953. He made the most of his time with the Sabre squadron, claiming six MiG-15s destroyed and two damaged between 16 May and 11 July. The 37th jet ace, Bolt was also the only Marine pilot to claim five or more kills in two wars (*Dean Abbott*)

MiG-15s! I told him to break hard left and down, while turning my flight into the MiGs. They broke right and down, and were out of sight almost immediately.

'My next job was to find the RF-80. I raised him on the radio and asked for his position. He told me he was still in a hard break to the left and down. We finally located him out over the water just south of the river. We stayed close to him all the way back, but the mission could have easily ended in disaster.

'My final missions were flown on the wing of Maj John Bolt, an exchange pilot from the Marine Corps. He was cut from the same cloth as McConnell with his aggressiveness, sharp shooting and good eyes.'

PEACETIME OPS

When the war ended, the F-86s from the 51st FW continued to maintain a heavy flying schedule, whether it was practising dogfighting out over the water west of Suwon or flying regular escort missions up the coast of Korea for twin jet RB-45s. Although these Sabres were loaded and ready to fight, they were not allowed to penetrate North Korean or Chinese airspace.

Many of these missions were tense affairs because MiG-15s flew parallel to them over land while the F-86s maintained their distance out over international waters. 1Lt James Lindsay was one of the 16th FS pilots who flew combat missions both during the war and immediately after the ceasefire;

'Once the combat missions were over, I experienced some of the best flying that a lieutenant could ever hope for. Since we had no enemy to shoot at, we had to keep ourselves sharp by flying training missions that included gunnery practice over water southwest of Suwon.

'It was not long before high command decided that a gunnery competition was a good way to keep the troops in a high state of readiness. This was set up between various squadrons at Suwon, Osan, Kimpo and Taegu. Needless to say, each wing was working hard to get their best shooters on their team. This entailed many training missions, using T-33s to pull the targets for these "top guns" so that they could sharpen their skills.

'Not being one of the best shots, and also being fairly junior in rank, I usually got the job of pulling the target "rag". I can tell you that some of those "top guns" were not all that good either! All I'll say is that some time the percentage of hits was mighty low, but that is another story.

'One day I was scheduled to fly the target ship, but this was a different sort of mission. I was to take off, fly out to the target area, declare a low fuel emergency and drop the "rag" at the closest airfield, which was Osan, and then head home. Well, I soon discovered why the "rag" was literally riddled with holes, since it had been used as a target at the gun harmonisation range the day before!

'The reason for this deception was to demoralise the competition when they saw the incredibly high percentage of hits in the "rag" that had landed on their airfield. It was hoped that they would be forced into giving up before the competition even started!

'However, what seemed like a good plan proved to be very ineffective. It took the boys at Osan AB only seconds to notice that all the holes in the rag were at near-90 degree angles – something that could only happen in a static environment. Despite the deception failure, I believe the 51st FW won the competition anyhow.'

All three squadrons within the wing stayed at Suwon for almost a full 12 months after the ceasefire due to the volatile nature of the truce with North Korea. The new pilots that rotated in with no combat experience were kept busy honing their skills, receiving guidance from the experienced pilots in case the war started again. This ensured that they would be able to stand their ground in the face of overwhelming odds, as had their predecessors.

The 16th FS left Suwon AB and moved to Misawa AB, in Japan, to perform air defence duties in July 1954. The following month the unit returned to its original base at Naha, on Okinawa, where it assumed all-weather duties. The 25th FS also returned to Naha AB in August 1954 from Suwon. Both of these units had, of course, been a part of the 51st FW pre-war.

1Lt John Winters walks to the flightline, ready to fly a mission over northwest Korea in early 1953. Carrying his parachute, mission maps and helmet, he is wearing a 'poopy suit' over his flying coveralls. The 'poopy suit' protected pilots that had to bail out over the frigid waters that surrounded much of Korea. Winters performed his combat tour with the 25th FS, claiming a solitary MiG-15 kill (on 12 July 1953) during his time in-theatre (*John Winters*)

Having been attached to the 51st in 1952, the 39th FS pulled out of Suwon in late July 1954 and was sent on a temporary basis to the 41st Air Division at Misawa AB for a year, before moving to Komaki AB, also in Japan. The 16th, 25th and 39th FSs had united under the command of the 51st FW and formed a group that proved to be more than a match for the communist fighter regiments equipped with the MiG-15. The wing had duly made a significant contribution to securing air superiority over the Korean Peninsula until war's end.

Col Robert P Baldwin had been the 51st FW's final wartime CO, and he had some very interesting comments to make about his wing, and its competition with the 4th FW;

'From a proving ground standpoint, we constantly learned a lot. This war will probably be the last "eyeball-to-eyeball" aerial conflict that this country will ever fight.

'I always felt that the 4th FW had a "personnel underground" at Nellis AFB that seemed to send its best "guns" to that wing. However, there was one time that this really worked in the 51st FW's favour. The training wing sent an unknown pilot named 1Lt Joseph McConnell to the 51st, and he arrived with no track record. At first, I could not believe he could be as good as what I had heard from other sources when I took command of the wing in January 1953. So one day, I assigned myself to

fly his wing. At the time, he and Maj Jabara were the top contenders for the crown of "ace of aces" in Korea, and I felt obligated to check him out. He had the most amazing eyesight and a real combat killer's instinct. Once he achieved position, he was a sharpshooter. I flew with him twice, and both times he shot down a MiG.

'The 4th FW had more kills than we did, but in the long run I believe that the 51st FW did the Air Force a better job in the experience mode because we averaged 90 pilots with combat experience and the 4th had only about 60.

'At the end of the day, both wings did an outstanding job against an enemy that had a numerically superior fighter force.'

Posing alongside the squadron CO's F-86F (note the command stripes on the jet's nose), 25th FS pilots 1Lts Bob Brackett and Henry Buttelmann smile for the camera during the summer of 1953 (*Bob Brackett*)

Within days of the ceasefire taking effect, the groundcrews at Suwon broke out the paint brushes and started adorning the F-86s' external fuel tanks with fancy paint schemes. When these same aircraft had been flying combat missions over 'MiG Alley' just weeks earlier, the likelihood was that the tanks would be dropped as soon as pilots were informed that MiG-15s were in the area. Painting these expendable items during wartime was, therefore, a waste of time. This all changed from August 1953 onwards. This airman from the 16th FS is decorating a Sabre drop tank at Suwon two weeks to the day after hostilities had ceased (*James Lindsay*)

39th FS stalwarts Lt Col George Ruddell (left), Capt Joe McConnell (centre) and Maj Clyde Wade (right) say their goodbyes as the 51st FW's 'ace of aces' prepares to board a US-bound transport aeroplane from Suwon at the end of his tour. McConnell left Korea as the top ace of the conflict, his request to remain in combat having been denied by senior Air Force officers in the Pentagon (*Larry Darst*)

In the final Fifth Air Force report submitted by its commander at the end of the war, Lt Gen Samuel E Anderson stated that the F-86 wings maintained air supremacy over North Korea through a combination of flying the greatest fighter the USAF had to offer manned by superior pilots who employed outstanding tactics. This was true to a certain extent, but the report went on to state that to believe that this was the sole reason the UN fighter force had prevailed would surely lead to a false sense of security in the future.

If you compared the air assets of the communists in Manchuria with those of the two Sabre wings in-theatre, air superiority was gained and maintained by a very small force that was always at a disadvantage. When you take these factors into account, it becomes obvious that the enemy contributed as much to its poor performance in the air as did the USAF. The consistent misuse of its capabilities, and a lack of skilled pilots in-theatre to exploit the outstanding attributes of the MiG-15, cost the communist regiments dearly.

The FEAF believed that the abandonment of large fighter formations in favour of small flights which maintained high cruising airspeeds and employed an aggressive offence had validity for future jet combat.

In January 1953 Col Robert P Baldwin assumed command of the 51st FW. Having flown P-38s during World War 2, he was one of the most experienced fighter pilots in-theatre by the time he reached Suwon. Baldwin duly became the USAF's 35th jet ace when he claimed his fifth victory while flying with the 25th FS on 22 June. His first kill had come three months earlier on 14 March during the course of a sortie with the 39th FS (*USAF*)

Col Malcolm E Norton took over the 51st FW from Col Baldwin in August 1953. He coordinated, and flew, numerous missions up to the mouth of the Yalu River and along the coast during the first few months of the uneasy peace that existed in Korea post-war (*Malcolm Norton*)

Legendary racing pilot and Thompson Trophy winner Roscoe Turner (centre) is surrounded by fighter aces from the Korean War during an airshow held at Dayton, Ohio, just weeks after the ceasefire had come into effect. The F-86s that the aces had flown to the event can just be seen at the top of this remarkable photo (*John Casey*)

The Fifth Air Force report also took into account the fact that the communists possessed a 'sanctuary' in Manchuria, and that they did not employ their full potential seriously enough to contest UN air superiority in North Korea, or UN air superiority over its many air bases in South Korea.

The various points in the USAF document also raise questions about what might have happened if that impressive MiG force had come down all at once in an all out attack on UN bases. They might have lost a significant number of aircraft during the course of the strike, but they would have dealt a great blow to the future of Sabre activity over 'MiG Alley'. Some 50+ years after the event, it is very easy to speculate 'what if'!

APPENDICES

Combat Chronology for the 51st FW (F-86 Sabre era) in Korea

1 November 1951
New F-86Es were loaded aboard the aircraft carrier USS *Cape Esperance* on this date for a fast trip across the Pacific Ocean, with a final destination of Korea and the 51st FW. The pilots that would man the two squadrons (16th and 25th FS) within the wing were also aboard

9 November 1951
The remaining 75 new F-86Es destined for the 51st FW were loaded aboard a second aircraft carrier, USS *Sitkoh Bay*, and sent to Korea

Late November 1951
The wing officially converted from the F-80C to the F-86E. All tactical operations with the Shooting Star ceased on 20 November

1 December 1951
The wing was declared operational when the 25th FS flew its first combat missions with the F-86E

6 January 1952
Six 25th FS pilots tried a new tactic and took their jets up to 45,000 ft over 'MiG Alley'. A large gaggle of MiG-15s came south of the river at 40,000 ft and failed to spot the Sabres prior to being bounced. Within two minutes the 25th FS had downed five jets and damaged three more. Maj Bill Whisner and Col Bud Mahurin were among those that scored

31 January 1952
The 51st FW finished the month with one of its best kill tallies, having downed 27 MiG-15s in January. This score would not be beaten until May 1953

23 February 1952
Maj William T Whisner became the 51st FW's first jet ace when he scored a single kill. The USAF's seventh jet ace of the war, his first two MiG kills had been scored with the 4th FW. Whisner had been a triple ace in World War 2

1 April 1952
Wing CO Col Francis Gabreski downed his fifth MiG to become the 51st's second ace

3 April 1952
The 16th FS's 1Lt Robert H Moore became the 51st's third ace. He was the USAF's ninth jet ace

6 April 1952
Capt Iven Kincheloe got his fifth kill to become the 51st FW's fourth ace. He was the USAF's tenth jet ace

22 April 1952
A flight of 25th FS Sabres, led by Capt Kincheloe, spotted a large number (24) of piston-engined aircraft concealed off the side of the runway at Sinuiju airfield in North Korea. The flight left several Yak-9s in flames, with many others riddled with 0.50-cal fire. It was the enemy's first major attempt to house aircraft on North Korean soil in several months

25 April 1952
Maj William H Wescott of the 25th FS shot down his fifth MiG-15 to make him the 51st FW's fifth ace and the USAF's 12th. He had only claimed his first kill on 1 April. Wescott's five-kill haul in just 24 days was one of the most outstanding records posted by a fighter pilot in Korea

31 May 1952
The combined combat sortie count for both Sabre wings reached a record high figure of 5190. A significant number of these missions were flown in support of fighter-bomber units, which had dramatically escalated their sortie tempo

1 June 1952
The 39th FS, after officially giving up its F-51D Mustangs to the 18th FBW, transitioned onto Sabres after being reassigned to the 51st FW. The unit's arrival at last brought the wing up to full three-squadron strength

21 June 1952
The 39th FS received four of the first six F-86Fs to arrive at Suwon. This latest Sabre variant would prove to be particularly formidable when flown by several of the unit's more aggressive pilots, as its high altitude performance was more on a par with the MiG-15bis than had been the case with the F-86E

23 June 1952
The 39th FS received two more brand new F-86Fs, boosting its complement to six

30 June 1952
June was a costly month for the 51st FW, with three Sabres being lost. MiG activity was down too, and only six were confirmed destroyed during the entire month

30 June 1952

USAF Intelligence determined that the fighter strength of the communist air forces worldwide had increased to the point where 22 air divisions could now be fielded. Each of these was the equivalent of one USAF wing (75 aircraft). Of the 1650 aircraft that equipped these divisions, more than 1000 were MiG-15s. A significant portion of these were based in close proximity to 'MiG Alley'

4 July 1952

The 39th FS's Capt Raymond W Staudte became the first 51st FW pilot to shoot down a MiG-15 whilst flying an F-86F

July 1952

The famous 'checkerboard' marking started to appear on the vertical stabilisers of all 51st FW F-86s. Its adoption finally made the wing's aircraft stand out from those flown by the 4th FW

August 1952

Three F-86Fs were fitted with the new solid leading-edge wing slats and tested in combat by 51st FW pilots. The positive results derived from these sorties led to all F-models in-theatre being modified to incorporate this feature

October 1952

The 502nd Tactical Control Group opened up a limited-scale air direction centre on Cho-do Island, off the west coast of North Korea. This gave the Sabre pilots ground-control intercept capabilities (radar) similar to those enjoyed by the MiG-15 pilots for so long

23 January 1953

Lt Col Edwin Heller, CO of the 16th FS, was shot down north of the Yalu River and became a PoW in China. At the time of his demise, Heller officially had 3.5 kills to his credit, and he had shot down a jet earlier in this mission but he was never able to submit proof. He survived captivity

16 February 1953

A lone Marine Corps F9F Panther made a crash-landing at Suwon after being hit by AAA over enemy territory. The pilot was Ted Williams, the professional baseball player (a future Hall of Fame inductee) having pulled a combat stint in Korea with the Marine Corps Reserves

21 March 1953

Capt Harold Fischer shot down his tenth MiG-15 to become a double ace

7 April 1953

Capt Harold Fischer was shot down over enemy territory. Like Heller before him, he too would spend the rest of the war in captivity. Fischer was not released until 31 May 1955

18 May 1953

39th FS flight commander Capt Joseph McConnell was credited with three kills in a day, raising his final total to 16 victories. He was immediately ordered to stand down and return home. McConnell was the top-scoring F-86 pilot of the Korean War, being one of only two triple aces to fly the Sabre. On this same date, McConnell's CO, Lt Col George Ruddell, shot down his fifth MiG to become the USAF's 31st jet ace

31 May 1953

A total of 77 enemy aircraft were shot down, with only a single F-86 being lost to enemy action in return. There were other Sabres that went down, but they were all attributed to operational causes

22 June 1953

Col Robert P Baldwin, commanding officer of the 51st FW, became the USAF's 35th jet ace of the war

23-24 June 1953

The 51st FW participated in one of the largest air strikes of the war when it escorted aircraft sent to bomb hydroelectric plants located deep in North Korea, close to the Yalu River. Sabre pilots protected 124 land-based fighter-bombers and aircraft from three carriers stationed off the Korean coast. The plants' power output capacity was reduced by 90 per cent. These attacks were carried out within 60 miles of 250+ MiG-15s sitting on the runway at Antung. There were no MiG kills listed during the two-day offensive

30 June 1953

The 51st set its monthly kill record for the war when it downed 29 enemy aircraft. 1Lt Henry Buttelmann (25th FS) became the USAF's 36th jet ace, and the youngest ace of the war (he was just 24 years old), during June when he downed five MiGs between the 19th and 30th of the month. F-86 pilots were credited with destroying at least 14 MiGs on this day alone, which set the one-day record for the war

22 July 1953

2Lt Sam P Young of the 25th FS downed the last MiG-15 to fall in the Korean War. This kill was also widely publicised in the US media as being the 800th MiG-15 to be shot down during the conflict

27 July 1953

The truce was signed, ending all hostilities. The 51st FW left a huge footprint on the list of statistics that summed up the UN efforts. From December 1951 through to 27 July 1953, the wing's pilots had accounted for 307 enemy aircraft destroyed, 285 damaged and 13 probably destroyed. Their kill ratio was an astounding 14-to-1. Fifteen pilots had also achieved ace status whilst flying 'checkertail' Sabres from Suwon

Aces of the 51st FW (In Order of Achieving Ace Status)

Maj William T Whisner Jr (7th jet ace of the war)
*** 15.5 confirmed kills in World War 2
25th FS Commanding Officer
Total kills – 5.5 (two kills with 334th FS/4th FW)
First kill on 8 November 1951
Final Kill on 23 February 1952

Col Francis S Gabreski (8th jet ace)
*** 28 confirmed kills in World War 2
51st FW Commanding Officer
Total kills – 6.5 (two kills with 4th FW)
First kill on 8 July 1951
Final kill on 13 April 1952

Capt Robert H Moore (9th jet ace)
16th FS
Total kills – 5 (one kill with 336th FS/4th FW)
First kill on 28 October 1951
Final kill on 3 April 1952

Capt Iven C Kincheloe (10th jet ace)
25th FS
Total kills – 5
First kill on 19 January 1952
Final kill on 6 April 1952

Maj William S Wescott (12th jet ace)
25th FS
Total kills – 5
First kill on 1 April 1952
Final kill on 26 April 1952

Maj Donald E Adams (14th jet ace)
16th FS
Total kills – 6.5
First kill on 20 January 1952
Final kill on 27 May 1952

Capt Cecil G Foster (23rd jet ace)
16th FS
Total kills – 9
First kill on 7 September 1952
Final kill on 24 January 1953

Capt Dolph D Overton III (24th jet ace)
16th FS
Total kills – 5
First kill on 22 January 1953
Final kill on 24 January 1953

Capt Harold E Fischer (25th jet ace)
39th FS
Total kills – 10
First kill on 26 November 1952
Final kill on 21 March 1953

Capt Joseph McConnell (26th jet ace)
39th FS
Total Kills – 16 (top-scoring ace of the war)
First kill on 14 January 1953
Final kill on 18 May 1953

Lt Col George L Jones (30th jet ace)
51st FW Commanding Officer
Total Kills – 6.5 (4.5 kills with 4th FW)
First kill on 1 October 1951
Final kill on 7 April 1953

Lt Col George I Ruddell (31st jet ace)
39th FS Commanding Officer
Total Kills – 8
First kill on 17 November 1952
Final kill on 19 June 1953

Col Robert P Baldwin (35th jet ace)
51st FW Commanding Officer
Total Kills – 5
First kill on 14 March 1953
Final kill on 22 June 1953

1Lt Henry Buttelmann (36th jet ace)
25th FS
Total Kills – 7
First kill on 19 June 1953
Final kill on 22 July 1953

Maj John F Bolt USMC (37th jet ace)
*** 6 confirmed kills in World War 2
39th FS
Total Kills – 6
First kill on 16 May 1953
Final kill on 11 July 1953

51st FW Overall Aerial Kill Statistics

By Squadron (totals include kills by exchange pilots)

16th FS – 90 kills, 12.5 probables, 125 damaged

25th FS – 112 kills, 10 probables, 109 damaged

39th FS – 103 kills, 8.5 probables, 78 damaged

51st FW – 9.5 kills
(kills made by pilots assigned to the Group or Wing HQ)

By Month

1951
December — 5

1952
January — 27
February — 10
March — 13
April — 22
May — 11
June — 6
July — 8
August — 12
September — 26
October — 12
November — 17
December — 11

1953
January — 24
February — 7
March — 8.5
April — 18
May — 23
June — 29
July — 12

Total **— 301.5***

* this total includes kills made by Marine Corps exchange pilots, but not those credited to RAF and RCAF exchange pilots

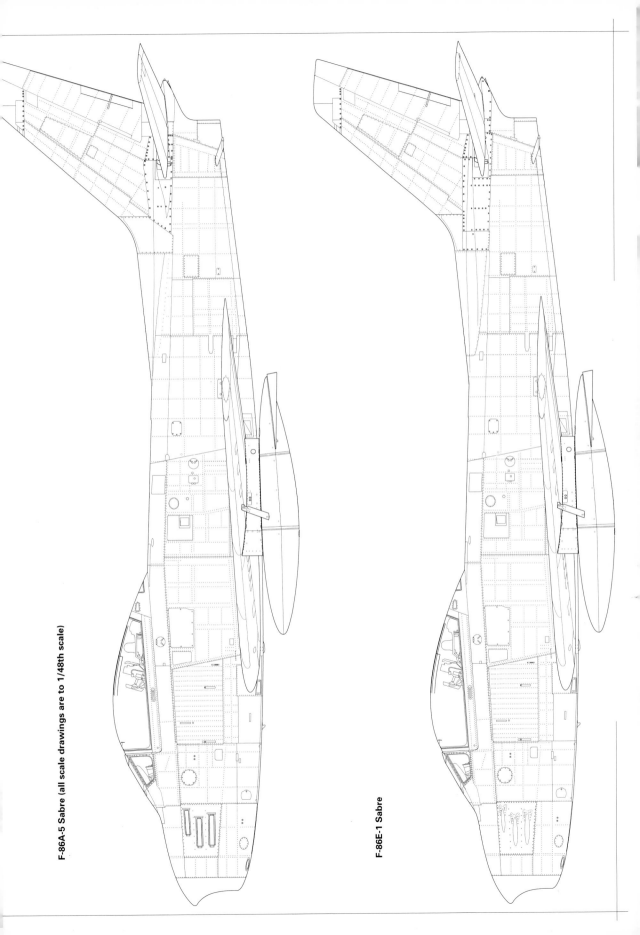

F-86A-5 Sabre (all scale drawings are to 1/48th scale)

F-86E-1 Sabre

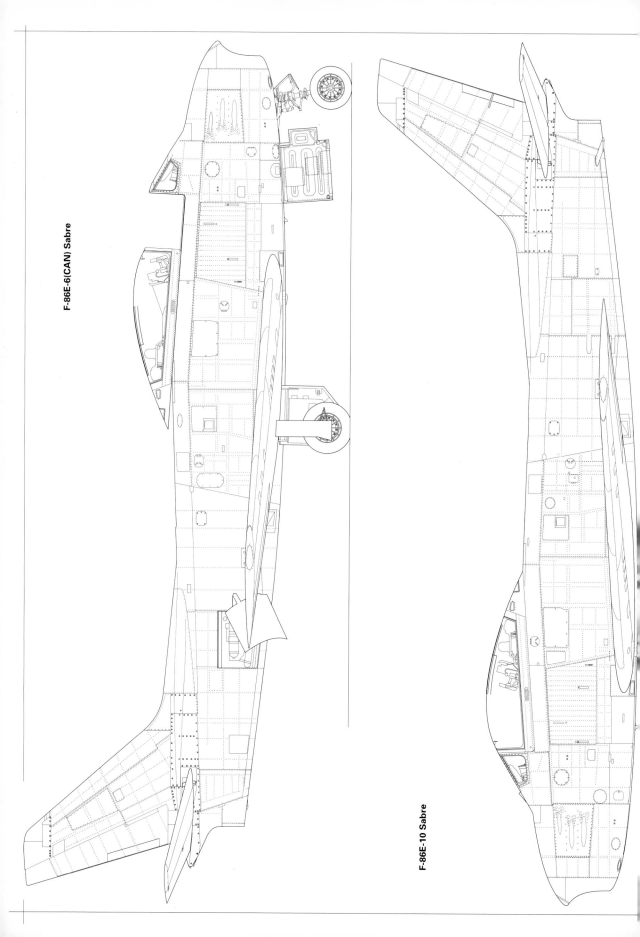

F-86E-6(CAN) Sabre

F-86E-10 Sabre

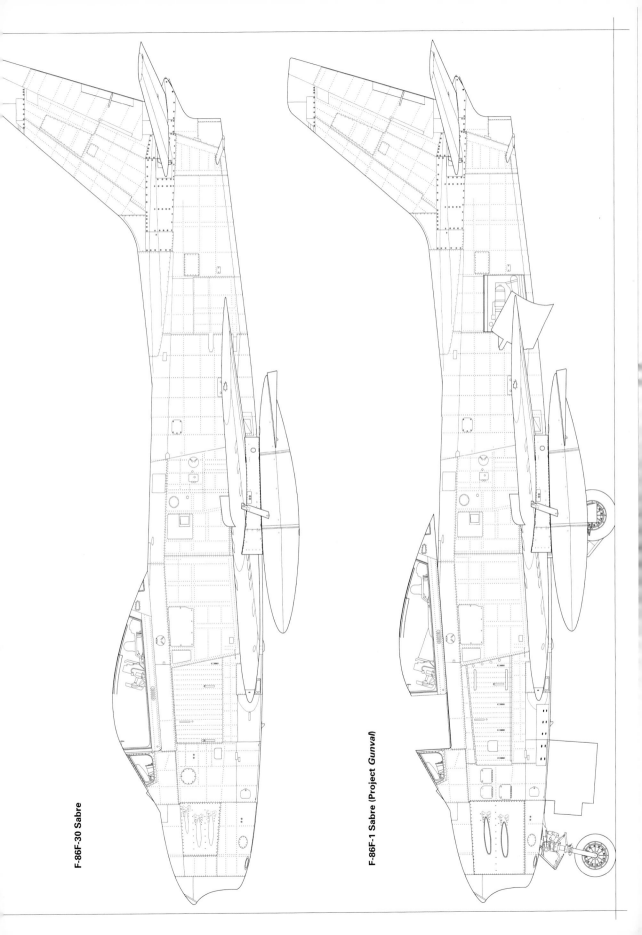

F-86F-30 Sabre

F-86F-1 Sabre (Project *Gunval*)

1

F-86E-1 50-598 *MY BEST BETT* of 1Lt Bernard Vise, 16th FS, Suwon AB, 1953

MY BEST BETT was an early model F-86E-1 that was assigned to the 51st FW at Suwon in late 1951. The blue stripe above the jet's checkerboard tail marking indicates that it belongs to the 16th FS. The fighter's designated pilot from late 1952 was 1Lt Bernard Vise, who, as a newcomer to the unit, flew as wingman for many of the squadron's top shooters in the final months of the war. 50-598 survived the war.

2

F-86E-1 50-624 *JO* of 1Lt Walter R Copeland, 25th FS, Suwon AB, 1952

JO was also amongst the first batch of F-86Es to be sent to the 51st FW when it converted from the Shooting Star to the Sabre in late 1951. Assigned to the wing for the duration of its combat tour, the aircraft's service records show that it was also flown by the 25th FS from Suwon during the immediate post-war period. One year earlier, it had been assigned to 1Lt Walter Copeland during the first few months of his combat tour. The name *JO* had already been painted onto the fighter's fuselage by the time Copeland arrived in-theatre. 50-624 was eventually transferred to the 35th FW in Japan in March 1954.

3

F-86E-5 50-649 *Aunt Myrna* of 1Lt Walter R Copeland, 25th FS, Suwon AB, 1952

F-86E-5 *Aunt Myrna* was delivered to the 51st FW in early 1952 as an attrition replacement. It was assigned to the 25th FS's 1Lt Walter Copeland that summer, and he used it to down his sole MiG-15 victory on 9 September 1952. The fighter also carried the names *Nancy* and *Jean* during its long combat tour in Korea. Although the victim of a minor flying accident whilst at Suwon, 50-649 was repaired and duly survived the war to be passed on to the 35th FW.

4

F-86E-10 51-2721 *THIS'LL KILL YA* of 1Lt Howard W Leaf, 25th FS, Suwon AB, 1952-53

25th FS F-86E-10 *THIS'LL KILL YA* was the personal mount of 1Lt Howard Leaf, although it was flown by several pilots from the 39th FS upon the completion of his combat tour in early 1953. Another jet to survive the war, 51-2721 ended up with the 199th FIS at Hickam Field, Hawaii, in December 1956. Leaf had already flown 100 missions in F-80Cs with the 8th FBG by the time he transitioned onto Sabres. Commanding the F-4 Phantom II-equipped 333rd TFS during the Vietnam War, he ultimately achieved the rank of Lieutenant General. Having amassed 5600 flying hours and completed 321 combat missions, Leaf finished his long and distinguished military career as Inspector General of the Air Force.

5

F-86E-10 51-2735 *Elenore "E"* of Maj William T Whisner, 25th FS, Suwon AB, 1952

Elenore "E" was assigned to World War 2 triple ace Maj William T Whisner of the 25th FS. He duly became the USAF's seventh jet ace of the Korean War whilst flying this machine, adding 3.5 MiG kills with the 51st FW to the two he had scored flying F-86As with the 4th FW's 334th FS in October-November 1951. His trio of victories with the 25th FS in January-February 1953 made him the 51st FW's first jet ace. Note that Whisner's aircraft lacks the wing's famous 'checkerboard' marking, the latter only being applied from July 1952 onwards. 51-2735 remained at Suwon long after Whisner had transferred home in March 1952, the jet surviving the war to also serve with the 35th FW in Japan.

6

F-86E-10 51-2737 *STEVEN RAY* of 1Lt Richard H Schoeneman, 16th FS, Suwon AB, 1952

F-86E-10 *STEVEN RAY* was also one of the first Sabres to fly with the 51st FW's 16th FS in Korea. A veteran of more than 18 months of combat flying, it was initially assigned to 1Lt Richard H Schoeneman as *STEVEN RAY*. He scored two and two shared MiG kills with the jet between March and May 1952. After Schoeneman finished his tour, 51-2737 was passed on to 1Lt Paul A Kauttu, who was credited with 1.5 victories whilst flying the fighter. It finally ended up with future 16th FS ace 1Lt Cecil Foster in early 1953, the latter having already scored several kills in 51-2738 (see profile 7) during the autumn and winter of 1952. 51-2737 was returned to the US and scrapped at McClellan AFB soon after the ceasefire.

7

F-86E-10 51-2738 *THREE KINGS* of Capt Cecil G Foster, 16th FS, Suwon AB, 1952

F-86E-10 *THREE KINGS* was made famous by ace 1Lt Cecil G Foster, who named the jet in honour of his three young sons. 51-2738 was all but written off in a collision with a wayward refuelling truck during a rain storm at Suwon in late 1952, the vehicle approaching the parked fighter too fast and skidding on the slick PSP matting as the driver attempted to take avoiding action. The truck hit the fighter side on, badly warping its airframe, and forcing 1Lt Foster to switch to F-86E-10 51-2737 (see profile 6). 51-2738 was eventually repaired and put back into service with the 25th FS as *"FATHER DAN"* (see profile 8). Post-war, it was one of a number of 51st FW jets to serve with the 35th FW.

8

F-86E-10 51-2738 *"FATHER DAN"* of Capt Floyd W Salze, 25th FS, Suwon AB, 1953

51-2738 was passed on to the 25th FS following its comprehensive rebuild in early 1953. Assigned to Capt Floyd W Salze, the fighter was christened *"FATHER DAN"* by its pilot in honour of the 51st FW Chaplain, Jesuit priest Dan Campbell. Salze was an exceptional pilot who had claimed two Me 262 kills in World War 2 flying P-51Ds. Quickly made a flight lead, he had destroyed two MiG-15s in *"FATHER DAN"* by early June 1953. Looking for his fifth kill during a mission over 'MiG Alley' on 11 June, his luck ran out when his jet (F-86F-5 51-2938) suffered an engine failure and Salze was forced to eject over the Yellow Sea. Although a rescue helicopter was soon on the scene, the Sabre pilot drowned before he could be winched to safety. *"FATHER DAN"* survived the war and was eventually transferred to the 35th FW.

9

F-86E-10 51-2746 *LADY FRANCES* of Maj Bill Wescott, 25th FS, Suwon AB, 1952

F-86E-10 *LADY FRANCES* was the personal mount of five-kill ace Maj Bill Wescott, who named it after his wife. He used several jets to claim his victories, and scored at least one in this particular aircraft. It was also periodically flown by Col Francis S Gabreski, CO of the 51st FW and a 28-kill ace from World War 2. Gabreski had already destroyed two MiGs with the 4th FW prior to arriving at Suwon. He would subsequently down a further 4.5 communist jets while leading the 51st, with his all-important fifth kill, on 13 April 1952, coming in 51-2746. Gabreski chose to fly with the 25th FS simply because the unit was combat-ready ahead of the 16th FS. Wescott also enjoyed success on 13 April, claiming two MiG victories. Although Wescott left the 51st FW in late August 1952 (after serving as CO of the 39th FS for two months), 51-2746 remained a part of the 25th FS until it was lost on 21 November that same year. The Sabre's pilot, 2Lt Peter D Blakely, ejected when he ran out of fuel after engaging a formation of MiG-15s that were attempting to attack F-84s just south of the Yalu River. Blakely landed on Cho-do Island and was quickly returned to Suwon.

10

F-86E-10 51-2756 *HELL-ER-BUST X* of Lt Col Edwin L Heller, 16th FS, Suwon AB, 1952

Wearing blue command stripes, *HELL-ER BUST X* was the personal mount of 16th FS CO Lt Col Edwin L Heller. An aggressive fighter pilot who had achieved ace status in World War 2 with five aerial and 15 strafing kills while flying with the 352nd FG, he sought out MiG-15s every time he headed north – often deep into Chinese airspace. All of his missions, except his final one, were flown in this aircraft, which he named *HELL-ER BUST* like his Mustangs in 1944-45. Having claimed two MiG-15s on 22 January, he pursued yet more enemy fighters some 150 miles into Manchuria in direct contravention to strict UN rules preventing such overflights. Hit by a well-aimed burst of cannon fire from a MiG-15, which broke his right arm and severely damaged the controls of his jet (F-86F-1 51-2871), Heller bailed out at low altitude and was captured. 51-2756 was written off in a crash on 20 July 1953.

11

F-86E-10 51-2762 *Elsie* of Col Clay Tice, 16th FS, Suwon AB, 1952

F-86E-10 *Elsie* was assigned to Col Clay Tice, who flew with the 51st FW for a short while as a Test & Evaluation pilot. Although he completed a number of combat missions with the 16th FS whilst in-theatre, Tice never got the opportunity to claim any MiG kills. One of the most decorated fighter pilots of World War 2, he was well known throughout the Air Force. Having flown P-38s in the Pacific while commanding the 49th FG in the final months of the Pacific War, Tice ended up commanding the Flight Test Center at Edwards AFB post-war. 51-2762 suffered a catastrophic engine failure near the mouth of the Yalu River on 6 June 1953, forcing RAF exchange pilot Flt Lt Ryan to take to his parachute – he was subsequently rescued.

12

F-86E-10 51-2791 *MY HUTCH* of 1Lt Kenneth L Palmer, 25th FS, Suwon AB, 1953

MY HUTCH was an F-86E-10 assigned to the 25th FS, as denoted by the red band above the checkerboard marking on the jet's vertical stabiliser. It was assigned to 1Lt Kenneth Palmer, and on 29 June 1953 he used the Sabre to shoot down a MiG-15. Originally issued to the 336th FS/4th FW at Kimpo AB in 1952, the aircraft spent the final months of the war with the 25th FS, before being transferred to the 35th FW.

13

F-86E-10 51-2795 *CHERYL JEAN* of the 16th FS, Suwon AB, 1952

The assigned pilot for F-86E-10 *CHERYL JEAN* remains unknown, as the jet was serving with the 16th FS at a time when the squadron had so many aircrew that a large number of its Sabres were flown by various different pilots. Things got so bad in mid 1952 that many of the newer arrivals were only getting ten hours of flying time per month. However, each aircraft only had one assigned crew chief, and he was allowed to have the name of his choice applied to the starboard side of the fuselage. This aircraft survived the war and was eventually transferred to the 199th FS at Hickam Field, Hawaii, in 1954.

14

F-86E-10 51-2816 *JOHNI'S JOY* of 1Lt Robert Moler, 16th FS, Suwon AB, 1953

F-86E-10 *JOHNI'S JOY* was assigned to 1Lt Robert Moler of the 16th FS in early 1953. Having been at Suwon since 1952, the aircraft was flown by several pilots over a 12-month period – its name changed with each new 'owner'! It survived in the frontline until war's end, and when the 16th FS pulled out of Korea it was passed on to the 35th FW.

15

F-86E-10 51-2832 *NINA II* of Col John W Mitchell (51st FW CO) and Maj John C Giraudo, 25th FS, Suwon AB, 1952-53

F-86E-10 *NINA II* was flown by several pilots in the 16th and 25th FSs, including Col John Mitchell – note the wing commander's stripes on the nose. When Mitchell was issued with F-86F-10 51-12950 (see profile 26) in early 1953, *NINA II* was passed on to Maj John C Giraudo of the 25th FS. He duly claimed two MiG-15s (on 13 and 14 May) destroyed whilst flying the jet. Giraudo was in turn shot down – either by a MiG-15 or AAA – in this aircraft on 16 June just south of the Yalu River. Following his release from captivity, Giraudo returned to the USAF and eventually retired with the rank of major general.

16

F-86F-1 51-2905 *"JEAN'S JOY"* of Capt Ralph L Stauffer, 39th FS, Suwon AB, 1952

One of the first F-model Sabres to arrive at Suwon in late June 1952, this aircraft was issued to the equally new 39th FS. Assigned to Capt Ralph Stauffer, who was one of the senior pilots in the unit, the aircraft had the name *"JEAN'S JOY"* applied to its starboard side by its crew chief. Directly opposite was the name *ELLA NARBY* – Ella was the name of Capt Stauffer's wife, who had just had their first child, whilst 'Narby' was short for 'and our baby'. The five kill symbols beneath the cockpit were credited to several different pilots that saw combat in the aircraft, as Stauffer failed to bag a MiG during his tour. The Sabre finished its career with the 39th FS in late 1954 when it was one of 320 F-models handed over to the Chinese Nationalist Air Force.

17

F-86F-1 51-2869 *LUCKY LADY* of the 16th FS, Suwon AB, 1952

Another early F-86F-1, *LUCKY LADY* was so-named by an unidentified pilot soon after its arrival at Suwon in June 1952. It was eventually reassigned to 16th FS pilot 2Lt Allen Enslen 12 months later (see profile 18). The right side of this aircraft displayed the titling *MY WONDERFUL GWEN* in very large lettering (see page 77), which earned it the nickname 'the flying billboard' amongst pilots at Suwon. When the war ended, 51-2869 was transferred over to the 4th FW, before eventually being passed on to the Chinese Nationalist Air Force in late 1954.

18

F-86F-1 51-2869 *JERRY* of 2Lt Allen Enslen,16th FS, Suwon AB, 1953

51-2869 had its long-standing nickname changed to *JERRY* soon after it was assigned to 2Lt Allen Enslen in June 1953. He used the veteran fighter to conduct a handful of combat missions up until the ceasefire, and then continued to fly it with the 16th FS post-war.

19

F-86F-1 51-2897 *THE HUFF* of 2Lt James L Thompson, 39th FS, Suwon AB, 1953

Arguably the most garish Sabre to see combat in Korea, 51-2897 was assigned to the 39th FS in the autumn of 1952. Having been used by several different pilots, the jet was allocated to 2Lt James Thompson in the early spring of 1953, and he used it down two MiGs in May and June of that year. The first of these kills saw him destroy a MiG-15 adorned with a large dragon motif on its left side. USAF Intelligence determined that this was probably flown by a high-ranking Russian pilot, and Thompson's mission report received special attention from senior officers within FEAF HQ. Soon after the mission, flown on 18 May, the fighter's crew chief, Sgt J W 'Bill' Manney, painted a dragon down the left side of the Sabre.

20

F-86F-1 51-2897 *Bill's Baby/MISS JERRY* of 2Lt James L Thompson, 39th FS, Suwon AB, 1953

The right side of *THE HUFF* also carried artwork and nicknames, which were also applied by the jet's crew chief, Sgt J W 'Bill' Manney. Probably the most photographed Sabre to see combat in the Korean War, the kill markings carried by 51-2897 were accumulated by several pilots. The aircraft was also supplied to Chinese Nationalist Air Force in late 1954.

21

F-86F-1 51-2910 *BEAUTIOUS BUTCH* of Capt Joseph McConnell, 39th FS, Suwon AB, 1953

This F-86F-1 was assigned to ranking Sabre ace Capt Joe McConnell throughout his time with the 39th FS. Seen here just prior to his triple victory haul on 18 May 1953, which made McConnell the USAF's leading ace of the war, the aircraft is adorned with 12.5 MiG silhouettes. These have been applied in an identical style to those used on squadronmate Capt Harold Fischer's F-86 (see profile 27). The spelling of *BEAUTIOUS* and the kill symbols were changed immediately after McConnell had claimed his final kills.

22

F-86F-1 51-2910 *BEAUTEOUS BUTCH II* of Capt Joseph McConnell, 39th FS, Suwon AB, 1953

McConnell's F-86F-1 is seen here after its nickname and kill tally had been modified following orders to this effect issued by FEAF HQ in the immediate aftermath of his 18 May 1953 exploits. Why these changes were made remains a mystery. McConnell never flew 51-2910 again after his triple MiG-killing exploits, as he had secretly exceeded his tour of duty by six missions in order to claim his final six victories. Once word of this unauthorised extension reached Lt Gen Barcus at Fifth Air Force HQ, he immediately grounded McConnell and cut orders for his return home. 51-2910 survived the conflict and was transferred to the 4th FW post-war.

23

F-86F-5 51-2941 *Little Rita* of 2Lt Richard Geiger, 16th FS, Suwon AB, 1953

F-86F-5 *Little Rita* was one of two jets painted with modified checkertails (see page 39) on their vertical stabilisers soon after their arrival in Korea in the summer of 1952. The non-standard markings did not remain on the jets for long, however. Initially assigned to the 39th FS, 51-2941 was transferred to the 16th FS before year-end, and it saw out the rest of the war with this unit. The Sabre's assigned pilot during the final weeks of the conflict was 2Lt Richard Geiger, who had the name *Little Rita* applied to its left fuselage in honour of his wife. Geiger joined the 16th FS very late in the war, and completed just seven combat missions in 51-2941 prior to the ceasefire coming into effect. He flew considerably more sorties with the aircraft post-war, before rotating out. The jet carried the name *Marcia Mine* on the right side of its fuselage. 51-2941 was transferred to the 4th FW in late 1953, and the Sabre eventually ended its flying career with the Chinese Nationalist Air Force.

24 & 25

F-86F-10 51-12940 *MIG MAD MAVIS* of Lt Col George I Ruddell, 39th FS, Suwon AB, 1953

Boldly marked with command stripes on its nose, *MIG MAD MAVIS* was assigned to 39th FS CO, Lt Col George I Ruddell. Its nose art was identical on both sides of the fuselage. Ruddell used this jet to claim his fifth MiG kill on 18 May 1953, thus becoming the USAF's 31st jet ace. That same day his 'D' Flight commander, Capt Joe McConnell, claimed his triple MiG haul to make him the leading ace of the war. Renowned for leading by example, Col Ruddell flew numerous combat missions and finished his tour with eight kills and four damaged. 51-12940 was also transferred to the 4th FW post-war, before ending up with the Chinese Nationalist Air Force.

26

F-86F-10 51-12950 *Mitch's Squitch* of Col John W Mitchell (51st FW CO), 39th FS, Suwon AB, 1953

F-86F-10 *Mitch's Squitch* was assigned to 51st FW CO Col Mitchell soon after its arrival at Suwon in early 1953. Mitchell had earned widespread fame throughout the Air Force for leading the 'Yamamoto Mission' on 18 April 1943, which resulted in the death of the architect of the Pearl Harbor raid. Having claimed 11 kills in World War 2 flying P-38s, P-39s and P-51s, Mitchell downed a further four MiG-15s (and damaged two more) whilst leading the 51st FW in this jet in 1953. 51-12950 survived the war and was eventually written off in an accident at Chitose AB, in Japan, a short while later.

27

F-86F-10 51-12958 *the PAPER TIGER* of Capt Harold E Fischer, 39th FS, Suwon AB, 1953

One of the top-scoring Sabres of the Korean War, 51-12958 was used to deadly effect by double ace Hal Fischer between 26 November 1952 and 21 March 1953. The 51st FW's second-ranking ace with ten kills, Fischer would have almost certainly scored more victories had he not been forced down over China on 7 April 1953 whilst flying F-86F-1 51-2852. Yet another 51st FW jet passed on to the 4th FW after the July 1953 ceasefire, 51-12958 also ended its days flying with the Chinese Nationalist Air Force.

28

F-86E-6(CAN) 52-2852 *DARLING DOTTIE* of Maj John F Bolt, 39th FS, Suwon AB, 1953

Canadair-built F-86E-6 *DARLING DOTTIE* was routinely flown by Marine Corps exchange pilot Maj John F Bolt during his combat tour with the 39th FS in 1953. A highly experienced fighter pilot who had 'made ace' with VMF-214 'Black Sheep' in the Pacific War, he was given command of Joe McConnell's crack 'D' Flight upon the latter's sudden transfer home in late May 1953. Bolt relished the challenge, scoring five MiG kills between 22 June and 11 July to become the 37th American jet ace. He was also the only F-86 exchange pilot ace of the war, and the only Marine to claim five or more kills in two wars.

29

F-86E-6(CAN) 52-2867 *CHODO-MATTE* of 2Lt Hans Degner, 16th FS, Suwon AB, 1952-53

Also Canadair-built, *CHODO-MATTE* served with the 16th FS for well over a year. Initially assigned to 2Lt Hans Degner, who gave the jet its distinctive nickname, the Sabre was later christened *Devil's Den II*. Degner finished his tour in early 1953 and rotated out of Korea. Subsequently flown by other 16th FS pilots during the course of its tenure, it is not known if the jet was credited with any confirmed kills.

30

F-86E-6(CAN) 52-2889 *Jeanie* of Capt Howard Leaf, 25th FS, Suwon AB, 1953

Canadair-built 52-2889 was flown by numerous pilots during its long career with the 25th FS, including Capts Howard Leaf and Duncan Morton. Just who was responsible for naming the fighter *Jeanie* remains a mystery, however. Its distinctive sharksmouth painted on the sides of its air intake denoted the jet's assignment to 'Tiger' Flight. When the war ended, very few of these war-weary E-models made it back to the US, most either being scrapped in Korea or turned over to the Chinese Nationalist Air Force in 1954.

31

F-86F-30 52-4550 *HAPPY GAY JOY* of Col William C Clark (51st FW CO), 16th FS, Suwon AB, 1953

52-4550 was assigned to Col William C Clark soon after he took over command of the wing from Col Mitchell on 31 May 1953. Although he did not register any kills in the jet, he regularly flew it over the Yalu River in the final weeks of the war. Like *Mitch's Squitch*, the Sabre boasts command stripes on the nose, but carries the 16th FS's blue tail stripe. Transferred to the 36th FBS/8th FBW post-war, where it carried the name *Sweet Miss Sylvia*, 52-4550 was eventually transferred to the Philippine Air Force in 1957.

32

F-86F-30 52-4584 *MIG MAD MARINE* of Maj John Glenn, 25th FS, Suwon AB, 1953

This F-86F-30 was flown by Marine Corps exchange pilot Maj John Glenn during his combat tour with the 25th FS in mid 1953, the future Mercury astronaut and senator using it to claim a trio of MiG-15s in the final two weeks of the war. A veteran of a previous combat tour in Korea flying F9F Panthers with the Marine Corps, Glenn's kills, like all the others credited to exchange pilots, never appeared in the USAF's official records for the 51st FW.

33

F-86F-30 52-4811 *Saber Dancer* of 1Lt Robert D Groszer, 39th FS, Suwon AB, 1953

Saber Dancer was one of the very last Block-30 F-model jets to be sent to Korea prior to the ceasefire. Assigned to the 39th FS in late June 1953 as an attrition replacement, the aircraft was flown by 1Lt Robert D Groszer. The latter had the name *Groszer's Gremlin* painted on the left side of the fuselage, although this was duly removed soon after the cessation of hostilities.

BIBLIOGRAPHY

Davis, Larry, *North American F-86 Sabre – Wings of Fame volume 10.* Aerospace Publishing, 1998

Dorr, Robert F, Lake, Jon and Thompson, Warren, *Osprey Aircraft of the Aces 4 – Korean War Aces.* Osprey Publishing, 1995

Fischer, Harold E, *Dreams of Aces.* Great Impressions Press, 2001

Foster, Cecil G, *MiG Alley to Mu Ghia Pass.* McFarland & Co, 2001

Futrell, Robert F, *The United States Air Force in Korea (1950-1953)*

Olynyk, Frank, *Stars & Bars.* Grub Street, 1995

Ravenstein, Charles A, *Air Force Combat Wings (1947-1977).* Office of Air Force History, 1984

Spurr, Russell, *Enter the Dragon.* Newmarket Press, 1988

Thompson, Warren E and MacLaren, David R, *MiG Alley.* Specialty Press, 2002

Wagner, Ray, *The North American Sabre.* Doubleday Publishing, 1963

Air Force Historical Research Center, *Korean War Victory Credits*

INDEX

References to illustrations are shown in **bold**.
Plates are shown with page and caption locators
in brackets.